# SAINTS
# AND
# POETS,
# MAYBE

# SAINTS AND POETS, MAYBE

## One Hundred Wanderings

### PETER W. YAREMKO

**Pamet River Books**
TRURO, MASSACHUSETTS

**Saints and Poets, Maybe**

by Peter W. Yaremko

PUBLISHED BY

**Pamet River Books**
Box 1160
Truro, Massachusetts 02666
www.pametriverbooks.com

ISBN: 978-0-9909050-3-5

Book Design: AuthorSupport.com

Manufactured in the United States of America

First printing

*For my Dears*
*Wendy and Julie*
*Erik, Connor, and Andrew*

# Contents

# *Preface*

With this book I've compiled in one place for reading and reflection one hundred of my favorite stories among the many I have posted during the past several years in my Paradise Diaries blog. There are many people behind my byline to thank.

First, the interesting personalities who populate these stories, without whom there would have been precious little to write about in the first place. And I also salute the many brilliant minds I quote throughout these essays.

Then there is Stacey Donovan, my astute editor. Shay Siegel's fresh set of eyes. Jerry Dorris at AuthorSupport.com. My eagle-eyed daughter, Julie, for proofreading and research, along with Deborah Cippola, who lent a hand from her perch in faraway Portland, Oregon. Wendy, my first-born and my energetic cheerleader, for her unflagging perseverance in pressing me to write. Finally my late wife, Jo Anne, the touchstone of my ambitions, and always the first to read my drafts and keep them—and me—real.

Most important, I thank the readers of this book. My hope is that you will find here writing that fuels your passion to live like you mean it.

Truro, Cape Cod, Massachusetts
September 2017

# Introduction

Ancient Celts had an affinity for the spirit world. They believed the threshold between seen and unseen was easy to traverse. They used to say that heaven and earth are only three feet apart. And in certain places the distance separating the two realms is even smaller. They called these the "thin places."

This Celtic sensibility seems to have been inherited by Charles Williams, who was a companion of C. S. Lewis and J. R. R. Tolkien in Oxford, England. During the thirties and forties these three intellectuals would meet each week to talk literature. Williams extended the concept of *co-inherence*, which Catholic theology had coined to define the human and divine natures of Christ and the relationship among the three persons of the Trinity. For Williams, the term included relationships among the interdependent components of God's creation that exist in mutual, innate relationship with one another. Visible and invisible are not in opposition. They are present simultaneously and they complete each other—as the tree is in the seed.

The late Anthony Bloom, a noted spiritual writer and hierarch of Russian Orthodoxy, explains how Williams' concept of co-inherence can affect us:

> *Living only in the visible world is living on the surface; it ignores or sets aside not only the existence of God but also the depths of created being. . . . But if we look deeper, we discover at the heart of things a point of balance . . .*

Eastern Christian spirituality has always been on easy terms with the invisible. More so than in the West, Byzantine spirituality demonstrates a pervasive acknowledgment and appreciation of a dimension beyond space and time in which we are immersed and to which we have access. Bloom, for example, called prayer "an exploration of this invisible world." He echoed Saint John Chrysostom, the fourth century archbishop of Constantinople and author of a Byzantine liturgy still in use. Chrysostom taught that, "When you discover the door of your heart you discover the gate of heaven."

Thomas Merton, the famed Trappist monk, was a devotee of Eastern mysticism. He came to recognize the gate of heaven everywhere: desert landscapes, towering mountains, awe-inspiring sunsets, stormy seas, starry nights.

Thin places are not confined to the physical. They also involve persons, events, things, ideas—even time. There also are thin places of the mind and of the soul where the earthly encounters the transcendent. Creation is permeated with the divine. Like "The Force" in the *Star Wars* movies, divinity embraces us and reveals itself if we let it. The veil between God's world and "our" world is often drawn back for a moment to give us a glimpse of the "beyond." Doesn't falling in love, for example, open to us a transfigured world? Doesn't love beckon us to a place beyond words, beyond ourselves—into illumination, enlargement, and transcendent mystery?

This idea was movingly apparent in Thornton Wilder's *Our Town*, the classic stage drama in which a deceased girl, Emily, is allowed to revisit a single day of her former life. As she does this, she notices how disengaged from life the living are and she asks the Stage Manager, the narrator of the play:

> EMILY: *"Do any human beings ever realize life while they live it?— every, every minute?"*

> STAGE MANAGER: *"No."* Pause. *"The saints and poets, maybe— they do some."*

The physical, spatial significance of thin places is known as *proxemics*, which studies how far apart we stand when we speak. Psychologists study the spatial requirements of humans and animals and the effects of population density on behavior, communication, and social interaction. Linguists study a culture for the symbolic and communicative role of spatial arrangements and variations in distance, as in how far apart individuals engaged in conversation stand, depending on the degree of intimacy between them.

In anthropology, the idea of occupying a space at one or both sides of a boundary is known as *liminality*, from the Latin word for "threshold." On the personal level, liminality involves breaking with previous practices, routines, or thinking. The ancient Romans underscored the significance of this transition by creating Janus—the dual-faced god of gates, doors, doorways, beginnings, and endings, for whom January is named.

Twilight, another example, is the liminal time, between day and night. *The Twilight Zone* television series offered this definition: "The middle ground between light and shadow, between science and superstition." The show's name is taken from an actual zone observable from space, where daylight or shadow advances or retreats around our planet. Noon and midnight are liminal, too, transitioning from morning to afternoon, from one day to the next.

We are in a thin place whenever we approach a threshold into a new reality or perception. We are altered in mind or psyche. This is why I like to think of myself as wandering the thin places of life . . . encountering and exploring Charles Williams's co-inherence . . . searching out Anthony Bloom's "point of balance" at the heart of things . . . striving to emulate Thornton Wilder's saints and poets who, maybe, "realize life while they live it." In doing this, I picture what Zora Neale Hurston described in her 1937 novel, *Their Eyes Were Watching God*. She likened love to the sea:

> *It's uh movin' thing, but still and all, it takes its shape from de shore it meets, and it's different with every shore.*

Our lives are like that, moving as they must while accommodating passing tides, currents, and eddies. But still and all, different with every shore.

# 1

## The Savage Goddess of Cape Cod

I heard it first from the lips of a chatty summer resident at Provincetown airport's departure gate: "Well, the time has come. I have to leave paradise."

Cape Cod? Paradise? I had been in the midst of research for my novel, *Little Flower: A Killing on Cape Cod*, which involves the real-life murder of a single mom several years ago. She lived down the road from my B&B in Truro, the narrow spit of sand near the outermost tip of Cape Cod. So I was very aware that the Cape has its obverse. Here's what I said about it in my book:

> *Jenny didn't know about the dour goddess of Cape Cod who inclines to protect her own at the expense of interlopers. The goddess's maternal pneuma harbors fragile plovers, soaring terns and raucous crows. She plays mother to fox and deer, to coyote and wild turkey, to bat and her-on. By her leave, doves—even robins—winter over. When nor'easters tear away her ocean beaches, she craftily persuades the Atlantic's own*

*currents to redistribute the displaced sand so as to lengthen the graceful*
*sweep of her bending hand at Provincetown.*

*But this same solicitous goddess can be savage to those not her own.*
*Each summer, her outstretched arm beaches whales and dolphins that*
*dare seek diversion in her waters. Each summer, she lulls scores of visit-*
*ing sea turtles to their death—Loggerheads, Greens and Ridleys. In*
*spring, they make their way north from the Caribbean for summer*
*feeding in Cape Cod Bay. As autumn sets in, many linger too long,*
*misled by the shallow Bay's warm comfort. Oblivious to the approach-*
*ing winter, they miss their chance to swim for the open ocean—and*
*safe passage south. As temperatures plummet in December, paralysis*
*overcomes the trapped turtles and they fall victim to "cold stun." The*
*numbed turtles are driven before the wind onto the beaches of Truro,*
*where impatient gulls do not grant them the grace of death before pick-*
*ing their eye sockets clean.*

From the first British settlers, who denuded Cape Cod of forests and
turned her into the planet's biggest sandbar, the desecration has been ceaseless. Noxious lead from the military base at Sandwich has percolated into
the mega-aquifer under Cape Cod. Female hormones, urinated into septic
systems, have been found in tap water. Airborne pollutants descend on Cape
Cod from smokestacks as far away as Illinois. The goddess relishes the ven-
geance she takes. Untold numbers of men, women, and children are estimated
to have drowned in her dangerous surrounding waters during the centuries.
And when women die at the hand of another—more than a half-dozen open
cases of murdered women remain—even then the goddess looks away.

Perhaps the dichotomy of Cape Cod explains why writers are drawn
to the creative vortex that defines this place—writers as diverse as Eugene
O'Neill and Jack Kerouac, E. E. Cummings and Norman Mailer. Lydia
Davis published a diary of her month's vacation in Provincetown—down
to detailing the footsteps of the tenant in the apartment above—along
the way winning a MacArthur Fellowship, a.k.a. the "Genius Award." And
from Thoreau came an entire book cataloging his Cape Cod ramblings.

I myself must keep writing if for no other reason than to deliver on what my B&B guests at The Sandpiper have signed up for—a stay in a writer's residence. I'm thinking about borrowing an idea from my neighbor. He's an artist, and during the summer months he turns himself into a tourist attraction by hanging out a shingle that offers visitors the opportunity to watch him paint—for an hourly fee. But I figure that watching an artist paint is dull enough; watching a writer write would be like watching the paint dry.

# 2

## *Spider-Man*

I once wrote speeches for the head of an IBM business unit whose go-to line when he screwed things up was "The staff let me down."

It was indicative of the low regard he had for the people who supported him.

An example. I was in his conference room with his chief of staff one afternoon, reviewing a draft, when a fly landed on the speech. The CEO whacked it with his bare hand and killed it. Then he flicked the fly's carcass with his thumb and forefinger—launching it directly into the chief of staff's eye.

"Did I get ya'?" he asked, gleaming with pride at his marksmanship, as the staffer daubed his tearing eye.

I enjoyed a moment of schadenfreude once when I watched Barack Obama standing embarrassed at the lectern because his staffer had failed to place the speech there beforehand.

Two things spoke to me as a speechwriter:

- The edge in Obama's voice when he twice called out to his "people"—which betrayed the pique beneath his attempt to make light of what was happening
- The speechwriter tripping as he dashed onstage to deliver the missing manuscript

When executives are on the podium, it's theater. It's their face that everybody's watching. The last thing a speechwriter wants to do is cause embarrassment.

On the other hand, Obama himself has owned up to the fact that "As president you're held responsible for everything, but you don't always have control of everything." It was a reminder of my own experiences with a couple of corporate speakers.

In one speech, the CEO promised his sales force that he would resolve the supply problem they were having with their manufacturing plant in Raleigh, North Carolina. I had given him a quick humor line to underscore the unacceptable performance of the manufacturing unit: "It's gotten so bad; they're telling Raleigh jokes in Poland."

Back in those days, neither the CEO nor I were sensitive to the fact that we were poking fun at the manufacturing people at the expense of persons of Polish descent. He got complaints about that line. But he took responsibility for the words I had put in his mouth. Our relationship remained strong, and I learned a big lesson—nothing teaches responsibility more than having someone put their trust in you.

Then there was the day a chairman of the board mistakenly started to deliver the wrong luncheon speech. His assistant had put into his three-ring briefing book as background another speaker's speech. The chairman read the entire first page before he realized his mistake. He simply turned to the correct tab, where he found his speech, and started over.

Afterward, he returned to his office and stayed behind closed doors for the rest of the afternoon. I don't know what he did in there, but he must have had a long, long talk with himself. Maybe it went something like Peter Parker's concluding soliloquy in the first *Spider-Man* movie: " 'With great power, comes great responsibility.' This is my gift, my curse. Who am I? I'm Spider-Man."

# 3

## *The Lady of the Dunes*

Rupert Holmes's one-hit wonder, "The Piña Colada Song," topped the charts as 1979 closed. The lyrics—"If you like making love at midnight, in the dunes on the cape"—capture the drastic societal change that took place during the turbulent two decades since Patti Page's 1957 paean to Old Cape Cod's "church bells chimin' on a Sunday morn."

Both tunes have combined to secure the popular image of Cape Cod as a beautiful paradise. But in the words of Provincetown Police Detective Meredith Lobur, "Beautiful places are not immune to brutal crime."

July 26, 2013, was the thirty-ninth anniversary of Massachusetts's most infamous unsolved murder, a cold case known locally as the Lady of the Dunes. On that morning in 1974, a young girl walking her dog on the dunes found a woman's naked and desecrated corpse lying face down on a towel with her clothes folded near her head. Her hands had been cut off and her wrists shoved into the sand as if she were doing pushups. The left side of her skull was crushed, her head nearly decapitated, and several teeth ripped out. In 2000, DNA was taken with no result. In 2013 investigators took another sample—exhuming the corpse discretely so as not to arouse notice.

Nothing came of the new DNA test, so here on Cape Cod, the Lady of the Dunes murder continues to haunt. Here's how I dealt with all this in my forthcoming novel, *Little Flower: A Killing on Cape Cod*:

"Things here are a little weird sometimes," Steve said.

"Like what?" Jenny asked.

"Like sometimes women are murdered here. And the cops never solve the murders. There's all these 'open' murder cases around here."

"Except Chop-Chop," Billy corrected. "They got Chop-Chop."

"Who is Chop-Chop?" Jenny asked.

"It was a long time ago," Billy said. "Nineteen sixty-eight. He was a pothead. Had a marijuana patch in his backyard. He killed two girls and cut them up and buried the parts behind his Mary Jane garden. That's why they called him Chop-Chop."

"That's what I mean about weird," Steve said. "Tell her about the Lady of the Dunes, Billy."

"That one's been open for what, twenty, thirty years?" Billy said. He turned to Jenny. "This one happened next door, in Provincetown. They find a woman out in the dunes on the ocean side. Her hands are missing. Her head's dangling off. The cops do a search of dental records. Nothing. They call her the Lady of the Dunes. Still open."

"Seems that all the open cases happen to involve women," Steve said. "A woman in Bourne stabbed to death in her bathtub. A teacher beaten to death in the woods in Mashpee. Another woman shot in the head in a parking lot in Provincetown. These were working people, you know? Not hookers or druggies."

"Hell," Danny said, "just last year a woman in her twenties goes for a job interview and disappears. Two months later they dig up her body from a beach in Sandwich."

"Like I say, weird stuff," Steve said.

# 4

## *WTF!*

During the summer months, driving from Manhattan to Cape Cod on I-95 involves a lot of stop-and-go. Out of sheer boredom I took notice of all the billboard advertising along this major artery between New York City and Boston. During my last trip, I realized that my reaction to most of the ad slogans came down to three letters: WTF!

Maybe you can do better than I in figuring out what these slogans are talking about:

- McDonald's: "You can't fake local flavor."
- 101.1 FM: "50 shades of radio"
- Coors Light: "First round, last call."
- Walgreens: "Well at Walgreens"
- Clean Care of New England: "We are the Grand Master of Disaster!"
- Mazda: "When you change everything, everything changes."

By the time I arrived home on Cape Cod, I was on a roll. Everywhere I looked, I was seeing ridiculous advertising:

- On my jar of peanut butter from Woodstock Foods: "Eat because it's good."
- A mailer from Duane Reade: "Treat your dog to a treat."
- And the punch line of Helloflo's tampon subscription service commercial: "Like Santa for Your Vagina."

What bothers me about these slogans is that they are self-obsessed, more in love with alliteration, internal rhyming, and parallelism than with communicating a persuasive thought. Advertising legend Bill Bernbach said it well: "Whereas the writer is concerned with what he puts into his writings, the communicator is concerned with what the reader gets out of it."

Another force in persuasiveness, David Ogilvy, backed him up: "What really decides consumers to buy or not to buy is the content of your advertising, not its form."

In other words, what you say in advertising is more important than how you say it.

# 5

## Starship Commanders

I've had the opportunity to work with two starship commanders. One was the hero of Apollo 13. The other the hero of TV's original *Star Trek* series.

During my years at IBM, Siemens, and Executive Media, my work as a speechwriter expanded to encompass writing and producing live corporate events. These were also known as industrial theater—recognition meetings, sales rallies, management conferences—for audiences ranging from a few hundred to more than ten thousand.

One of the benefits of being a producer is that the job enabled me to indulge my fantasies. In creating program content that would excite and motivate audiences, I was influenced by my boyhood passion for science fiction. I had watched *Captain Video* on my family's black-and-white DuMont and deported myself as one of his Video Rangers. I was there in the theater for the premieres of the 1950s sci-fi movies that are now classic: *The Thing . . . Invasion of the Body Snatchers . . . The Day the Earth Stood Still.*

Fast-forward to the early 1990s, when it was a natural for me to hire Jim Lovell, whose heroic performance brought the crippled Apollo 13 and its crew safely home. He served as on-camera narrator of an identity video for the high-tech ROLM Corporation, which pioneered voice mail among other telecommunications innovations.

I got to pick him up at SFO; I noticed how he put on his seat belt first thing. And as we drove down Route 101 past Moffett Field, I listened to him reminisce about testing planes tethered to an anchor post inside one of Moffett's vast hangars. In the car that day, I asked Captain Lovell the question that had burned since my days as a Video Ranger: "Just how strong is the thrust you feel when you lift off?" His disappointing answer: "About the same as accelerating a car." Heck! Captain Video had led me to believe the acceleration of liftoff practically flattened your eyeballs.

Captain Lovell was a delight to work with—affable, patient, and a natural on camera. I hired him a second time to speak to a ROLM recognition event about his Apollo 13 experience.

Then there was Captain Kirk . . . William Shatner. You remember: "To boldly go . . ."

On stage in front of six hundred or so top performers at a different ROLM recognition event, the CEO—a German—talked with a video-projected Captain Kirk, who was supposedly orbiting Earth in the *Starship Enterprise*. Then, using what's known as a laser-cone effect, we "beamed" Shatner down to the stage to join the CEO and help him conduct the awards ceremony.

Shatner turned out to be a not-so-good choice. He toyed with the CEO and kept going off prompter. The CEO was trying to follow a carefully crafted script to help him with what was his second language. To his credit, the CEO, who happened to hold a doctorate in engineering, prevailed.

The difference between the two spacemen? One of these starship commanders was a real hero. The other only played one on TV.

# 6

## *Corporate Hara-Kiri*

Watching Beyoncé shatter mirrors in Pepsi's "Live for Now" commercial reminded me of the night my wife became a casualty of the Cola Wars that have been going on since the 1980s.

Jo Anne was working as an event manager at a Pepsi show in Palm Springs. If you've ever produced an event for one of the cola companies, you know the *de rigueur* routine Jo Anne followed. She made sure the food and beverage department served only Pepsi drinks at meals, and she directed soda and snack machines throughout the venue to be switched over to Pepsi products. If there was an exposure in the plan, it was the banquet act—the Beach Boys. Their rider stipulated Diet Coke as part of their backstage catering. So Jo Anne's team wrapped the Boys' Coke cans in colored paper to conceal the names and logos.

Everything went swimmingly until the evening ended—when client kudos were anticipated.

As soon as the hundreds of happy Pepsi sales reps filed out of the ballroom, the show crew had begun breaking down the set.

Load-out was well under way when one of the Pepsi executives wandered into the ballroom. She, of course, was the only one to notice that sitting on the lip of the bare stage was an open can of Coca-Cola that one of the show crew had carried with him from backstage. The crew froze when they heard the aghast Pepsi gal shouting at Jo Anne about this unforgiveable breach.

At moments like this, there is nothing for an event planner to do but fall on her sword. This ritual suicide by disembowelment with a sharp knife, you may recall, was practiced in Japan by samurai as an honorable alternative to disgrace. It was known as hara-kiri—belly cutting.

Of course, what Jo Anne really wanted to do was yell back at the Pepsi gal, "What the hell's in a name? They all taste the same!" When you think about it, she had a point. The cola companies have always inflated their advertising with the magnificent jargon of consumer marketing.

During the past half century, both cola companies have flailed about trying to define the persona of their respective sugar-water products. I counted almost two dozen Coke slogans since 1961. Pepsi deployed fewer during the same period. But they were as oblique as, say, Coke's "Life Tastes Good" (introduced in 2001 and resurrected in 2013).

Here's a sampling of Pepsi's slogans:

- "Now It's Pepsi for Those Who Think Young"
- "You've Got a Lot to Live, and Pepsi's Got a Lot to Give"
- "Pepsi's Got Your Taste For Life"
- "Pepsi. The Choice of a New Generation"
- "Be Young, Have Fun, Drink Pepsi"
- "Right Now"
- "Generation Next"
- "For Those Who Think Young"
- "Live for Now"

In introducing its 2013 campaign, Pepsi's press release called it, "the next iteration of Pepsi's 'Live for Now' brand spirit, which encourages fans to embrace the NOW and be at the epicenter of, and helping to define, pop culture."

Huh?

# 7

## *A Boy Named Josh*

My advanced snorkeling class had gathered in a gazebo overlooking the beach at Columbus Landing Park on the paradise island of Grand Turk. It was the afternoon session on the second day of our eight-day course.

We were students of Melon Dash, founder of Miracle Swimming, which specializes in teaching adults to overcome their fear of deep water. Our class routine was to hold a discussion period of ten minutes to a half hour or more, during which we would talk through the plan for the class, voice any concerns or fears we might have, and set some goals for what we wanted to accomplish in the next couple of hours. After instruction in the water, we would gather again to process what we just learned—experiences, breakthroughs, aha moments . . . whatever.

Except that this week, we came to know a little boy we will remember for a long time.

We had decided as a group to swim out to a reef farther from shore than any of us had ever ventured. It was marked by an orange buoy that I couldn't even see from the beach. The return swim would be against the current, so as much as it sounded like a fun thing to do, we were a bit antsy. Chris Canaday, our Miracle Swimming instructor for this class, had just begun to facilitate the opening discussion period. And then along came Josh.

Josh lived on this capital island of the Caribbean nation of Turks and Caicos. At eleven years of age, he was a chest-thumping seventy pounds of uninhibited attitude. With him was his cousin, Silvano, and a pack of eight feral dogs—known as Royal Bahamian Potcakes. Garrulous Josh was obviously the alpha—of the pack, of Silvano, and probably of his entire neighborhood.

Josh bounded into the gazebo, shouting a loud, authoritative command for the Potcakes to remain out. Silvano was allowed in. The gazebo is public, so there was nothing we could do to preserve the privacy of our discussion period. The two boys joined us on the bench that wrapped around the interior of the gazebo and listened to Chris describe what our trip to the buoy would entail. For about fifteen seconds.

In his gravelly voice—much louder and deeper than his small frame would seem to house—Josh commenced to help Chris facilitate. He warned us of Shirley the Barracuda . . . of ugly octopuses . . . of a schoolmate who had drowned in these waters. Just what we needed to hear. Then—dismissing a core Miracle Swimming principle—Josh said, "Why don't you stop talking about it and go do it!" Just what Chris needed to hear.

As will happen with children, familiarity took over; Josh helped himself to one of my fins and tried it on for size. Then my wife's fin. Then he hung on Chris's arm.

Chris cut the discussion period short, and the boys followed us into the water. They did dolphin dives around us as we industriously tried to get into our snorkel gear. They asked if they could try our snorkel masks, and each of us said no.

But here's what happened . . . and why I am writing about Josh today.

When we returned from our swim to the reef, Josh and Silvano were waiting for us in the gazebo. This time they listened attentively as we spent a few minutes discussing our lesson. When we finished, Josh took Chris's hand . . . took my hand . . . Silvano took my other hand ... and my wife's hand . . . and our group joined hands because Josh told us to.

With no embarrassment or awkwardness, this macho little man said we were going to pray now. And in his deep voice and his Creole accent, Josh offered the most articulate prayer that I, for one, have heard in a long time. He thanked God, whom he called "Father in Heaven," that we had been able to swim to "the booby" and return safely. He prayed that we would come back to Grand Turk so we could all see each other again.

I found out later that everyone in our small group had worried that while we were in the water, Josh and his cousin would surely rummage through our belongings in the swim bags. We each admitted feeling guilty of unfairly and wrongly judging the boys. The next day, my wife and another student went to the dive shop and purchased two snorkel sets—expensive ones that neither boy could hope to afford.

I had more than a snorkeling lesson that day: "Amen, I say to you, unless you turn and become like children, you will not enter the kingdom of heaven. Whoever humbles himself like this child is the greatest in the kingdom of heaven." (*New American Bible,* Matthew 18: 3,4)

# 8

## *Top Ten Things I Didn't Do on Cape Cod This Summer*

1. Lie on the beach
2. Get a tan
3. Lose weight
4. Acquire a Golden Labrador (or any other dog)
5. Watch the Independence Day Boston Pops concert on TV
6. Try to make a left-hand turn against traffic
7. Eat lobster stew served by a window with an ocean view
8. Make love at midnight on the dunes
9. Make love at midnight
10. Make love

Any explanation I offer—busy with work, busy with guests, busy with travel—sounds like what it is. An excuse.

But heck! Isn't the history of the Internet one of missed opportunities? The major record labels allowing Apple to take over the digital music business? Blockbuster refusing to buy Netflix for a mere $50 million? The Excite online service company turning down the chance to acquire Google in 1999 for $750,000?

Aren't cult movies basically the ones Hollywood missed—that the fans made successful?

Despite the missed opportunities, there is an Internet anyway.

Despite the missed opportunities, Hollywood continues anyway.

Despite *my* missed opportunities of the summer of 2013, wait until next summer!

# 9

## *Goddess of the Hunt*

Fifty-three hours of blue-water swimming . . . 110 miles from Cuba to Florida . . . five tries over three decades. It was just about thirty years ago that I was on a first-name basis with the living legend who is Diana Nyad.

I had just been named chief communications officer for IBM's newly launched software business unit, and I was pulling together the unit's first conference for seven-hundred-some managers. I hired Diana to be our motivational speaker. It was 1985 and Diana Nyad, then in her mid-thirties, had become a national celebrity for her twenty-eight-mile swim around Manhattan in less than eight hours in 1975. She had already made her first attempt at the Cuba–Florida run in 1978. When that effort failed, she followed a year later with a successful 102-mile swim from the Bahamas to Florida in twenty-seven hours.

I no longer recall exactly what she said at our 1985 conference, but I do vividly remember two things about her as she sat beside me in the front row waiting to give her talk:

- Her beautiful legs as sculpted as a Greek statue from untold hours of flutter kicks in pools and oceans
- And, unseen by the audience, her pre-speech jitters

It was an odd thing to observe how someone as courageous as Diana Nyad—someone accustomed to being on the professional speaker circuit all those years—could be so nervous about getting up on stage. After all, her very name summons up images of strong females of antiquity. *Diana,* for example, was the name of the Roman goddess of the hunt. And *Nyad* was explained in a *Newsweek* story:

> *When she was around six years old, her stepfather [Aristotle Nyad] showed her the word naiad (the original spelling of the family name) in a dictionary. The time, she stated, was "just at the juncture when I was developing an ego, the id of self-definition. The first meaning of naiad: 'from Greek mythology, the nymphs that swam the lakes, fountains, rivers and seas to protect them for the gods.' The second meaning: 'girl or woman champion swimmer.' Aris winked at me, and we both understood that this was my destiny.*

I guess we have to call to mind Jerry Seinfeld's unforgettable stand-up routine about the stress of public speaking: According to most studies, he says, people's number one fear is public speaking. Number two is death. This means if you go to a funeral, you're better off in the casket than doing the eulogy.

During the years since Diana Nyad spoke to our IBM conference, she went on to be a respected media reporter and commentator. And in 2013 she made her career dream come true when she shuffled onto the shore of Key West. In overcoming four Cuba-to-Florida setbacks and in dealing with her fear of public speaking, Diana Nyad surely followed her own mantra: "All of us suffer heartaches and difficulties in our lives. If you say to yourself, 'find a way,' you'll make it through."

# 10

## *Gateways*

Contemporary poet Lia Purpura suggests that where we were before we were born and where we are when we're "not anymore" might be very close . . . might be the same place. The Celts held a similar idea ages ago. They used to say that heaven and earth are only three feet apart and that in the "thin places" the distance is even smaller.

I have to believe Stonehenge was one of the thin places they had in mind—their idea of a gateway to beyond. There is also a thin place on the island of Vieques reminiscent of Stonehenge. A quarter mile down a rutted dirt road into an isolated jungle area near the town of Esperanza, you can find a scene that stinks of spirituality. Boulders huger than houses rest in concentric circles—signaling a gateway that seems too perfectly drawn. To add to the mystery, four thousand-year-old human remains were discovered at this crude site some years ago; they were relocated to San Juan for safekeeping.

These ancients might have intuited something modern physicists currently postulate. Parallel dimensions. Extra universes. Multiverses.

Physicists have detected the shapes of parallel dimensions by examining the influence these dimensions exert on the cosmic energy released in the big bang. The existence of parallel dimensions is a key element of string theory. The idea that everything in the universe is made of tiny, vibrating strings of energy is the leading contender for a unified theory of everything.

String theory suggests that the world we know is not complete. In addition to our four familiar dimensions—three-dimensional space and time—string theory predicts that additional, hidden spatial dimensions are curled in tiny geometric shapes at every single point in our universe. The theory of everything would unify quantum mechanics and gravity—but it would require extra dimensions of space.

In *Conjectures of a Guilty Bystander,* Thomas Merton claims "the gate of heaven is everywhere." Unspoiled landscapes. Regal mountains, sunsets and starry nights.

Like parallel universes, paradise is more intuited than seen. Tourists, for example, abandon Cape Cod as winter approaches because they don't see—or even seek—those contours of paradise that are evident only in winter. Seals warming themselves on unpeopled beaches. Sea smoke rising off frigid waters in phantom silhouettes. Lake-effect snow off Cape Cod Bay drifting down from sunny skies.

Visitors to my other paradise, Vieques, avoid coming here during the autumn rainy season. As a result, they don't get to see the electrically charged side of paradise—lightning storms that ride the horizon in fearsome parades of energy. Thunder so hammering that you can actually feel sound.

Paradise can be found everywhere, all right. Because paradise is in the eye of the beholder.

# 11

*Lonely, or Alone?*

*The rate of loneliness in the U.S. has doubled since 1980.*
**—University of Chicago study**

During the familial celebrations of Thanksgiving and Christmas, Cape Cod restaurants record their busiest day of the year with visitors seeking to spend Thanksgiving in a place reminiscent of Pilgrims. In Vieques, Christmas week sees guesthouses full up, premium high-season rates, and rental vehicles in short supply. At the same time, those forced into strained, pseudo celebration with extended family will find these holiday weeks stressful if not downright excruciating.

It's at this time of year that we are reminded of those among us who don't enjoy trusted relationships in which affection can be given and returned. These are not only alone. These are lonely. Edward Hopper, whose Cape Cod summer house is within sight of my home in Truro, was preoccupied with depicting loneliness. Almost every critic sees in his mature paintings solitude, alienation, loneliness, and psychological tension.

As early as 1923, Hopper titled an etching *The Lonely House*. The composition includes two children, the title suggesting a larger kind of isolation—one that's embedded in our society.

Then there's Hopper's *Macomb's Dam Bridge*, painted in 1935. It depicts New York, a city of millions, with no people in it. "It's probably a reflection of my own loneliness," he commented. "It could be the whole human condition."

Not only did he show in his paintings melancholy solitary figures, but he also drew trains and highways—metaphors for escape. "To me the most important thing is the sense of going on. You know how beautiful things are when you're traveling," Hopper said.

So what is "loneliness"? Is a person who is alone also a person who is lonely? Experts tell us being alone is healthy when it is a choice. When it is the result of occurrences beyond our control—bullying, empty-nesting, bereavement, unrequited love, loss of friends or loved ones—being alone can become being lonely. Existentialist philosopher Michele Carter has this take:

> *Loneliness is not the experience of what one lacks, but rather the experience of what one is. In a culture deeply entrenched in the rhetoric of autonomy and rights, it is ironic how much of our freedom we expend on power . . . on conquering death, disease, and decay, all the while concealing from each other our carefully buried loneliness, which, if shared, would deepen our understanding of each other.*

Novelist Thomas Wolfe connects the intense loneliness of his own life to a universal aspect of humanity:

> *The whole conviction of my life now rests upon the belief that loneliness, far from being a rare and curious phenomenon, peculiar to myself and to a few other solitary men, is the central and inevitable fact of human existence.*

The University of Chicago study:

*Lonely individuals are more likely to construe their world as threatening, hold more negative expectations, and interpret and respond to ambiguous social behavior in a more negative, off-putting fashion, thereby confirming their construal of the world as threatening and beyond their control. These cognitions, in turn, activate neurobiological mechanisms that, with time, take a toll on health.*

And of "being alone"? Is it necessarily lonely?

Not for Sister Wendy Beckett, the Catholic nun we know from her PBS series about classic paintings. Even within her cloistered convent, she chooses to live, pray, and write in solitude—as a hermit who occupies a trailer that sits apart from the nuns' main building—having no social intercourse with her sisters.

*Our language has wisely sensed these two sides of man's being alone. It has created the word "loneliness" to express the pain of being alone. And it has created the word "solitude" to express the glory of being alone.*

That's Paul Tillich, the theologian and philosopher whose writings inspired Martin Luther King, Jr. Tillich adds, "The courage to be is the courage to accept oneself in spite of being unacceptable."

Now there's something to think about during the holiday season.

# 12

## *Let's Strangle Siri!*

When I worked at IBM's development laboratory in Poughkeepsie in 1968, I wrote about the company's efforts in speech-to-text. The development engineers told me speech-to-text would be a long time coming. Now, with the Speech Interpretation and Recognition Interface embodied in the newest versions of iPhone, such an advance seems facile.

I bought myself an early Christmas gift—an iPhone—at the Cape Cod Mall in Hyannis. I'm looking forward to getting back to Vieques to give Siri a run for her money with questions like, "Which of the thirty-six Puerto Rican holidays are we celebrating this week?" and "Are the ferries from Fajardo running on time today?"

As with any emerging technology, Siri is taking her share of lumps. She's been dissed by late-night comics and suffered jabs on *The Simpsons*. Al Pacino reportedly stomped his iPhone into pieces in a Hollywood eatery a few summers ago during a fit of anger at Siri. Even Steve Jobs wasn't entirely happy with her. He didn't like the name, but he couldn't come up with a better one before launch.

From what I've read, it seems that Dag Kittlaus, one of the founders of the original Siri application purchased by Apple, named the service after a woman he worked with in Norway. In Norwegian, *siri* means "beautiful woman who leads you to victory." But in Portuguese *siri* means "*crab.*"

Before you give your kid a Siri-enabled iPhone for Christmas, think again. Because of calculators, lots of young people can't do arithmetic. Because of word processing, schools are walking away from the teaching of cursive writing. And—guaranteed—Siri will cause proper punctuation to become as obsolete as diagramming a sentence.

Just speak naturally and Siri understands you. Instead of typing, tap the microphone icon on the keyboard. Then say what you want to say and iPhone listens. Tap Done, and iPhone converts your words into text. All that's true. Siri can search the web for you. She can place phone calls for you. She can even spell the spoken word *supercalifragilisticexpialidocious.* But she can't punctuate! You have to tell Siri where and what type of punctuation you want to use in your messages—by speaking the punctuation during the composition of your message.

For example, to get Siri to write this:

*Hi, how are you? Did you see the game last night!?*

You have to speak this:

*Hi comma how are you question mark did you see the game last night exclamation point question mark.*

If I wanted to dictate the title of this chapter, I would have to speak:

*Caps on let's strangle siri exclamation point.*

Can you imagine any kid on Planet Earth doing this?

Young people—most of whom already know less about punctuation than they should—will speak their messages without a thought to punctuation. As a result, their messages will appear as one, long, run-on sentence. We will enter an era of stream-of-consciousness writing worthy of James Joyce. If you dare to criticize them for their ignorance and their laziness, their defense will be, "Oh, everybody knows what I mean."

# 13

## *Dark*

*Our fantastic civilization has fallen out of touch with many as-*
*pects of nature, and with none more completely than with night.*
*Primitive folk, gathered at a cave mouth round a fire, do not fear*
*night; they fear, rather, the energies and creatures to whom night*
*gives power; we of the age of the machines, having delivered our-*
*selves of nocturnal enemies, now have a dislike of night itself.*

**—HENRY BESTON,** *THE OUTERMOST HOUSE: A YEAR*
*OF LIFE ON THE GREAT BEACH OF CAPE COD,* **1928**

In Truro, a fifty-mile drive east–northeast from mainland Massachusetts, we suffer sunset at 4:12 on December 21, the shortest day of the year— and the longest night.

Night visits special terrors on some. Here's how I described one such night of torment in my forthcoming novel, *Little Flower: A Killing on Cape Cod:*

*The darkness of Jenny's bedroom was as absolute as an amusement park horror house, and the quiet of the place was as deep as its darkness. The only sound she heard was the gush of her own pulse where her ear pressed the pillow, and she shifted her head to silence the cadence. She drew up her knees and tugged the duvet high on her face. She knew her wide-awake mind would start racing with overwrought scenarios and exaggerated rages—all the incubi that had become nocturnal visitors since her breakup with Eater.*

For others, as Rod Serling wrote, "There is nothing in the dark that isn't there when the lights are on."

Many find dark a place of transcendence. Vincent van Gogh was one: "I often think that the night is more alive and more richly colored than the day."

If we agree with Henri Matisse that "a picture must possess a real power to generate light," we have to ask—what about dark? What power must a painting possess to depict dark? Van Gogh answered the question in 1888, painting *Starry Night over the Rhone* at night and directly from nature.

Terror, transcendence—even humor—can be found when we toy with day and dark, light and night. The late George Carlin, for instance, is credited with joking, "Why is it called 'after dark' when it really is 'after light'?"

So what is dark? Is it after light? Is it absence of light? Is the difference between light and night nothing more than one letter of the alphabet? Why the eternal joust between light and dark?

Fearing the descent of endless, unmarked days of darkness, J. R. R. Tolkien published *The Hobbit* in 1937—on the eve of World War II. The second installment of *The Hobbit* movie trilogy crystallized Tolkien's anxiety: "No light, Wizard, can overcome the darkness."

Some eight hundred years ago, Francis of Assisi glimpsed a different outcome in the contest between light and dark. Christmas was his favorite day, and in 1223 he conceived the idea of celebrating Christ's birth by reproducing the Bethlehem manger scene in a church at Greccio, Italy. It was he who gave us the devotional tradition of the crèche that brightens so many homes and places of Christian worship during this Christmas season. And it may have been Saint Francis who promised us, "All the darkness in the world cannot extinguish the light of a single candle."

# 14

## *Light*

*There are two kinds of light—the glow that
illuminates, and the glare that obscures*

**—JAMES THURBER**

This might explain why Catholics burn Advent candles during
December to commemorate the arrival of the child they acknowledge as the Light of the World. Homes and businesses are decked out with
glaring electric luminescence, but it's the glow of the candle that matters
at Christmas.

Here on Cape Cod, light has always been a part of the character of the
place. In my forthcoming novel, *Little Flower: A Killing on Cape Cod,* I
tell the story this way:

*At least two hundred fifty generations of Native Americans had lived
on Cape Cod before the Europeans eliminated them. These indigenous*

31

*dwellers took as their name Wampanoag: People of the First Light.
They were isolated from neighboring tribes. With no human contact
beyond their borders, their belief was that they saw each day's sun-
rise before anyone else. So they thought themselves a chosen people. It
wasn't until the year 2000 that a study determined exactly where in
the United States the sun's first rays fell each morning. The Wampanoag
believed correctly.*

Cape Cod's unique light is legendary; it is a significant reason why so
many people have tagged this transcendent sandbar "paradise." This is
especially true of the countless artists Cape light has attracted for more
than a century. Our light made the Outer Cape—Wellfleet, Truro, and
Provincetown—home to the nation's oldest art colony and a microcosm
of American twentieth century art. Why? Because—to paraphrase French
novelist Paul Bourget—light is to painting as ideas are to literature.
Cape light has been described by painters as reminiscent of the South of
France or the Greek islands. The artistry of Hans Hoffmann helped spark
Abstract Expressionism. Hoffmann founded a Provincetown art school
that attracted innumerable painters, many of whom went on to make significant contributions to American art. He taught that, "In nature, light
creates the color. In the picture, color creates light." Imbuing a painting
with light is no easy matter. "Light is a thing that cannot be reproduced,
but must be represented by something else—by color," Paul Cézanne said.
"Light does not exist for the painter."

Cape Cod's winter light is no less spectacular than summer's.

"The light in winter is most varied; there are days when it's clear and
bright, carving the earth into light and shadow like a razor," landscape painter
Peter Fiore says. "Yet, at times, the light can be soft and quiet as a whisper,
with color of the most intense chromatic variations anyone could ever need."

I can attest to that. The most beautiful sunsets I witness from my home
in Truro occur in winter. Perhaps this is one of the reasons why the Arts
Foundation of Cape Cod and the Cotuit Center for the Arts held a combined winter exhibit in the melancholy depth of our winter. It was titled
*Seeing the Light.*

# 15

## *The Ecology of Self*

I once had an acquaintance of many years whom I thought I knew well. But when his wife died, I was startled to learn that this guy didn't know how to do his own laundry or book his own travel or even manage his own checkbook. He was a partner in a thriving dental practice, but he couldn't care for himself.

When I was a young man studying for the Catholic priesthood, I was fortunate to have as our seminary rector a farsighted monsignor who instilled in us the belief that we had to learn self-sufficiency in preparation for the solitary life of a parish priest. So we spent each Saturday laboring to maintain our "house." I learned to make up my bed in military fashion, to wash windows without leaving streaks, to handle a bulky floor-buffing machine.

I know an untold number of guys—at least in my older age demographic—who require someone to take care of their day-to-day needs because they cannot or will not maintain themselves.

This is the "*un-maintenance man.*"

On the other hand, all the women I know are highly self-sufficient. Not one suffers the malady of un-maintenance. My widowed daughter, for example, can jump a car, install appliances, and make sense of the snake's nest of cables that link cable box, monitor, DVR, and DVD.

I spent most of my first year in Vieques alone, house-sitting a friend's place while our house was being built. When I moved down to Vieques, my wife was concerned that my nutrition would suffer because—although I could make a mean chili, bake hearty breads, and serve up a full Ukrainian Easter dinner—I was not in the habit of preparing three meals a day. But I learned—and learned well enough to open a bed-and-breakfast and see my guests posting Facebook photos of their breakfast plates.

Caring for yourself, cleaning up after yourself, taking responsibility for managing your daily living—these are salutary and enriching practices that form what I call the *ecology of self.*

They also are precepts of the ancients. Confucius, for example, is said to have warned that the father who does not teach his son his duties is as guilty as the son who neglects them. The Buddha engendered the worth of taking responsibility for ourselves and for the environment we occupy. Saint Paul counseled the Galatians—and us—that "each will have to bear his own load." [Galatians 6:5]

Now, take heed. There might be a downside to all this. *The American Sociological Review* in 2013 reported a study showing that when men did certain kinds of chores around the house, couples had less sex. Specifically, if men did *all* that the researchers characterized as feminine chores such as folding laundry, cooking, or vacuuming—the kinds of things many women say they want their husbands to do—then couples had sex 1.5 fewer times per month than those with husbands who did what were considered masculine chores, like taking out the trash or fixing the car. It wasn't just the frequency of sex that suffered, either—at least for wives. The more traditional the divisions of labor, meaning the greater the husband's share of masculine chores compared with feminine ones, the greater his wife's reported sexual satisfaction.

After I read about this study, I informed my wife that I wouldn't be doing any more housecleaning because it might adversely affect our sex life. She says she doesn't mind a dirty house.

# 16

## *Lighting the Match*

2014 marked a half-century since a twenty-two-year-old boxer named Cassius Clay won the world heavyweight boxing championship.

He was challenging Sonny Liston, who had never lost a match and was considered perhaps the best heavyweight boxer in history. In a poll of sportswriters before the fight, 43 of 46 picked Liston to easily beat the trash-talking upstart. But it was Clay's moment. Against all odds, he won.

The only reason I was mindful of this anniversary is that I came across it while researching a speech for a client. One of the benefits of being a speechwriter is the continuing involvement I have in the thought processes, experiences, and ambitions of the intelligent and interesting executives I write for. These are successful people, and by my vicariously getting into their minds, my own life gains added dimension.

This time, a speech I was writing was speaking to me. In thinking about the way Cassius Clay seized his moment, I questioned why so many of us sleepwalk through life. Marcel Proust recognized this common malady:

"In theory one is aware that earth revolves, but in practice one does not perceive it, the ground upon which one treads seems not to move, and one can live undisturbed. So it is with Time in one's life."

Didn't I need to be shaken awake—like the young men on the 1980 USA Olympic hockey team? They were thought to have no chance against the powerful Soviet Union team. But the USA coach told his amateurs, "You were meant to be here. This moment is yours."

"I'm not going to hit the ball out of the park every time I'm at bat—I understood that," revered baseball player Mickey Mantle is famously quoted. "During my 18 years, I came to bat almost 10,000 times. I struck out about 1,700 times and walked maybe 1,800 times. You figure a ballplayer will average about 500 at-bats a season. That means I played seven years without ever hitting the ball."

But my every action should be aimed at some worthy outcome, shouldn't it? Isn't opportunity for achievement embedded in each day? Whether it's career or lifestyle or love? As I pass through my days, shouldn't I be as alert to opportunity as a stalking cat? Doesn't the architectural design dictum counsel us always to "think of the next larger thing?" The act of identifying or imagining or fashioning the next larger thing in our lives is itself a form of fulfillment. A life can be a work of art, constantly being shaped and reshaped like a kaleidoscope that must be touched to bring forth its beauty.

Mia Hamm was the brilliant 2004 Olympic soccer gold medalist. I read and reread the quote I had included in my client's speech until Mia's words sounded like a haiku:

*I am building a fire.*
*And every day I train, I add more fuel.*
*At just the right moment, I light the match.*

It's not too late for me to start maintaining this kind of positive attitude in the game of life, I think. Remember the old joke about the Little League team that was losing 10 to nothing in the first inning?

One of the fathers who were sitting behind the losing team's bench quietly called to his son, "Don't be discouraged, buddy." The boy turned and answered, "I'm not. We haven't been up to bat yet."

# 17

## *Grandma's Lost Doughnuts*

Until she died, my grandmother wore her hair in the peasant braid popularized by Yulia Tymoshenko, the former prime minister of Ukraine released from prison in the wake of the regime change in Kiev. But, unlike Yulia, Thecla Smytana was an actual Ukrainian peasant. In 1911, at nineteen years of age, she spoke no English and possessed no skills beyond the kitchen. But this illiterate farm girl somehow got herself six thousand miles to the United States, where she found work cooking and cleaning for well-to-do families in Manhattan—and tasted meat for the first time.

She was a hard-as-nails, pull-yourself-up-by-your-bootstraps woman who loved me dearly and had an immense influence on my life. While my parents were at their jobs, I spent long days in her Staten Island kitchen keeping her company as she cooked and baked. She told me the folk stories of the old country and sang the songs she learned as a girl. She'd let me use an overturned tumbler to cut dough circles that she formed into the stuffed patties called *pyrohy* in Ukrainian. At sunset, she went about the house turning on lights and reciting in a loud whisper her prayers against the night, which she'd memorized as a girl. But more than anything, she shared with me the central mantra of her own life: *Treba zmusyty sebe.* You have to push yourself.

Calvin Trillin is said to have once joked, "The most remarkable thing about my mother is that for thirty years she served the family nothing but leftovers. The original meal has never been found."

That wasn't true of my grandmother. She cooked an array of Ukrainian dishes, most centered on vegetables that grow in or close to the soil—potatoes, beets, cabbage. Peasant cuisine, you say? Ha! A rose may look prettier, but cabbage makes a better soup.

When my aunts and uncle returned home from their office jobs in Manhattan every evening precisely at seven, a fresh meal was waiting for them. And for dessert were the jelly doughnuts. *Pampushky.*

Grandma made them from scratch. Deep-fried and sporting a thick coat of granulated sugar. In my little-boy eyes, they were as big as softballs. James Beard may have said that good bread is the most fundamentally satisfying of all foods. But I say stuff it with jelly and see what happens. Paradise.

My idyllic time alone with Grandma ended when I started kindergarten. I began the business of growing up, and it wasn't until I was a young man and Grandma was gone that I realized I had never thought to ask her to teach me to make *pampushky*. Her three daughters never asked, either. As first-generation immigrants, they distanced themselves from their Eastern European heritage because they so wanted to be "American."

I know Grandma would have given the recipe to me if I had asked for it. But I never did.

Grandmothers as a species don't write down their recipes. After all, as author Linda Henley says, "If God had intended us to follow recipes, He wouldn't have given us grandmothers." My grandmother's dishes were not written down because she didn't know how to write. And whatever magic yielded those unforgettable doughnuts, it went to the grave with her.

# 18

## The Slowness of Time

*The grandfather had become very old. His legs would not carry him, his eyes could not see, his ears could not hear, and he was toothless.*

*When he ate, bits of food sometimes dropped out of his mouth. His son and his son's wife no longer allowed him to eat with them at the table. He had to eat his meals in the corner near the stove.*

*One day they gave him his food in a bowl. He tried to move the bowl closer; it fell to the floor and broke. His daughter-in-law scolded him. She told him that he spoiled everything in the house and broke their dishes, and she said that from now on he would get his food in a wooden dish. The old man sighed and said nothing.*

*A few days later, the old man's son and his wife were sitting in their hut, resting and watching their little boy playing on the floor. They saw him putting together something out of small pieces of wood. His father asked him, "What are you making, Misha?"*

*The little grandson said, "I'm making a wooden dish. When you and Mamma get old, I'll feed you from it."*

*The young peasant and his wife looked at each other and tears filled their eyes. They were ashamed because they had treated the old grandfather so meanly, and from that day they again let the old man eat with them at the table and took better care of him.*

**"The Old Grandfather and His Little Grandson"**

**—Retold by Leo Tolstoy**

My grandson, Connor, spent his spring break from Drexel University with my wife and me and came away smitten with the paradise that is Vieques.

We had lots of time together, and he and I talked of how each of us likes to think of ourselves as out-of-the-ordinary personalities. When other kids in kindergarten built structures, for example, Connor knocked them down. When my kindergarten teacher passed around a large can of sugared gumdrops and told us to each take one, I took two.

As Connor grew from a little boy to a fascinating young man of many talents and interests, we both discovered even more similarities.

Not only does he look like I did as a youth, but we both:

- Tan easily
- Drink our coffee black
- Hate drinking soda
- Prefer water
- Like spicy food
- Enjoy the taste of lemon
- Hum to ourselves when preoccupied
- Have a birthmark in the same spot on our right ear
- Choose yellow when confronted with a color choice
- Have had the quality of our writing acknowledged
- Had identical chain-reaction car accidents on the highway—with our vehicle totaled and no injury to ourselves

Each time Connor and I discover a common trait, we rush to be the first to pronounce, "Another similarity." The line always brings us a laugh.

But I've listed only some obvious similarities. I have yet to learn how much else I may pass to Connor in the way of perceptions and principles.

I may never know.

Erasmus Darwin, for example, died without knowing how much he influenced his more famous grandson, Charles, in their surprisingly similar theories of evolution and inheritance.

In a 2012 study of fifty-five hundred grandparents in eleven European countries, Norwegian sociologist Knud Knudsen found that Europeans generally spend a good deal of time with their grandchildren. Grandmothers are more involved with their grandchildren when a couple is younger, he said, but with age, grandfathers usually show greater solicitude.

It seems to be all about *time*.

One's time is one's greatest gift to a loved one, especially for a grandfather—whose inventory of it is running down.

Here's writer John Clarke:

*I think I know now why there can exist a special bond between grand-fathers and their grandsons. I think it has to do with their perceptions of time. Somehow we in the middle have either forgotten or have become so world-weary that the slowness of time seems like a long-ago dream. Einstein was the first to work out the math about time. He was able to mathematically prove something we all somehow already know: that time is not a constant. I personally believe that time slows then speeds up and then slows again over the course of our lives. I remember well the long days of my childhood when I had nothing more important to do than to sit on the porch with my grandfather and hear him tell the story about how a beehive works or how to graft a branch onto an apple tree. He and my maternal grandmother were the only adults I knew who understood this slowness of time. They proved this by making time for me.*

# 19

## *The Sounds of Silence*

Paul Simon is said to have conceived his famously poetic ballad "The Sounds of Silence" in the middle of the night, in his bathroom, with the lights out and tap water running. No wonder he had to closet himself like that in order to create. It's about the only way to get away from the modern world's ceaseless cacophony of noise, piped-in music, and ubiquitous babble.

Even paradise is noisy. In Vieques, for instance, roosters cock-a-doodle-doo through the night and dogs bark around the clock. On Cape Cod, April brings crocuses, the openings of shops and restaurants, and the arrival of tourist mobs lugging what Dr. Seuss would call their floofloovers and tartookas, their pantookas, their dafflers and wuzzles.

I served my writing apprenticeship in the city rooms of daily newspapers, so I'm no stranger to noise. I learned how to block out chatter, shouting, and cursing while putting together a news story accurately and succinctly (well, at least succinctly). But wherever I go, I can't seem to escape the latest madness-inducing caterwauling—the vapid pop music that saturates stores, shopping malls, airports, and almost every other public space. I am forced to endure the wailing of panty-less Miley Cyrus even while I pump gasoline!

To seek a higher, truer—and quieter—paradise, I went on a week's retreat to Saint Joseph's Abbey, the Trappist monastery in Spencer, Massachusetts. This monastery is Cistercian of the Strict Observance, the order founded in the twelfth century that was home to the late, famed, Catholic priest and spiritual writer, Thomas Merton, who wrote in *The Monastic Journey*: "Monks must be as trees which exist silently in the dark, and by their vital presence purify the air."

Silence is supreme at the abbey from the time the monks rise near three in the morning to begin their day of prayer and work. They speak only when necessary and not at all from 8 p.m. to 8 a.m.—the period known as the *Grand Silence*. Meals are eaten together, but in silence. Visiting guests, like me, follow the regimen. What's the point of all this hush? To give God a chance to get a word in.

It can be puzzling at first, because if we read Psalm 29, it seems that we can't escape the voice of God:

*The voice of the Lord flashes forth flames of fire*
*The voice of the Lord shakes the wilderness of Kadesh*
*The voice of the Lord makes the oaks to whirl and strips the forests bare*
*The God of glory thunders*

It seems that the voice of God is earth-shatteringly loud.

And it can be—if you listen for it in silence.

The prophet Elijah, for example, sought God in windstorm and earth-quake and fire—all the places that the people of his time expected God might be found. But Elijah heard God only as a "still, small voice."

In Psalm 46, the Creator himself advises us to "Be still, and know that I am God."

For the Trappists, the quiet helps them maintain near-constant focus on God, whose language is silence. In silence, the monks listen for the voice of God. In joining them in the silence of my week there, I sat quietly and tried to rid my mind of its incessant interior monologue, and I turned my full attention to the present moment. I was alone with my own measured breathing . . . the sharp knocking of hot water pipes . . . the overhead drone of an airplane . . . the soft shuffle of monks' sandals along tiled cloister floors . . . early spring birdsong outside the window . . . the muffled flutter of a moth's wing against a lampshade.

These are the sounds of life around me. I cannot help but *hear* them. But what I *listen* for are the inner sounds of silence. The ones words can't capture. And in doing that, I share in a small way the monk's quiet, lifelong quest—a finite creature searching inwardly to find the infinite.

# 20

## *Born into Eternity*

For the past two decades I have watched my firstborn grandson, Erik, grow from a six-pound squirt to a strapping and achingly handsome young man. Sporting a handful of my genes, of course, he competes in triathlons. A week after he ran his first marathon, Duquesne honored him with a double degree in biology and physical therapy cum laude.

How did all this happen so fleetingly and so emphatically? Where did the time go? What is time, anyway?

It brought to mind a truism quoted by Anaïs Nin, the French-born novelist whose 1931–to–1974 diaries track her voyage of self-discovery: "We don't see things as they are, we see them as we are."

Aha, I thought. So *that's* what happened. I was still seeing Erik as the baby who inspired me to run my first marathon. In 1991, here's how I wrote about Erik's role in my marathon:

*The build-up to the race was in the news almost daily. Whenever I heard or read about it, I felt my nervousness rise. I hadn't run farther than fifteen miles and according to my training regimen, I still needed to do two long runs of eighteen miles and one of twenty miles. But because of the lost weeks, I had time left to do only one eighteen-miler. I decided to try for it that weekend and if I made it, I would definitely attempt the marathon.*

*But Sunday morning came, and I was able to do only 17 miles. Afterward, I was sore from the waist down. My hip joints hurt. All the muscles in my legs were burning. My feet felt so tender it hurt even to walk. One toenail was bruised black. Even my butt muscles were in pain. To run another nine miles—what it would take to complete the marathon that was now only two weeks away—was inconceivable. I decided to drop out.*

*When I went to the office the next day, I walked down the hall to tell my coworker, Madeleine, about my decision. She had run two marathons herself, and on this morning she was a woman without pity.*

*"What's your grandson going to say someday," she asked, "that his grandfather thought about running a marathon?"*

*The dark side of hubris is humiliation. My daughter had just delivered our family's first grandchild. To drop out of the race at this point would mean my grandson would be left the legacy of a loser, the remembrance of a grandfather too timid even to try.*

*So on November 3, 1991, there I was at the starting line on Staten Island, harboring the secret that I was not ready to run the marathon.*

But run it I did—wearing a singlet on which was silkscreened THE GALLOPING GRANDPA. I crossed the finish line to be greeted with a medal around my neck, a rose in my hand, and tears in my eyes.

So what, then, is the truth about time? Here's Augustine of Hippo speaking to us from the fourth century: "If no one asks me, I know what it is. If I wish to explain it, I do not know." He goes on to say, "How can the past and future be, when the past no longer is, and the future is not yet? As for the present, if it were always present and never moved on to become the past, it would not be time, but eternity."

The only explanation is that we are beings born into eternity. And that is explanation enough.

# 21

## *Star Stuff*

At the height of his popularity, the astronomer Carl Sagan was a guest presenter at an IBM sales recognition event in Bermuda, where I was writing speeches and continuity for the corporation's executives. During a break in the program one afternoon, Carl and his wife, Linda, held hands as they trekked up a windy bluff overlooking the Atlantic Ocean. When they reached the top, an immense grin shone on his face as he took in the expansive view of the sea below. That image of Carl and his wife helps me understand what he meant when he wrote, "For small creatures such as we the vastness is bearable only through love."

Of course, Carl was referring not only to the planet's seven seas but also to the immensity of the universe. He popularized his thinking in his famous television series, *Cosmos*. There he proclaimed:

*The surface of the Earth is the shore of the cosmic ocean. On this shore we've learned most of what we know. Recently we've waded a little way out, maybe ankle deep, and the water seems inviting. Some part of our being knows this is where we came from. We long to return. And we can. Because the cosmos is also within us. We're made of star stuff.*

Now, many years after I met Carl, I travel back and forth between my homes on Cape Cod and Vieques—both prime places in which to enjoy striking views of the night sky. Truro, Cape Cod's least-populated municipality, is more than a fifty-mile-drive from mainland Massachusetts and has little ambient light to obscure the night sky. The same is true of sparsely populated Vieques, the little island off Puerto Rico. In both places, it's hard to be outside at night and resist the temptation to stargaze. Although these two tiny points on the planet are separated by nearly two thousand miles, their views of the star canopy are virtually identical, leading me to feel that I am "home"—no matter which of my two houses I happen to be in.

I didn't understand this feeling until I recently came across something written by American author and longshoreman Eric Hoffer. He suggested that our preoccupation with the sky, the stars, and a God somewhere in outer space is a homing impulse. "We are drawn back to where we came from," he wrote.

Van Gogh described his nighttime painting of stars as a religious experience.

And as I take in the night sky, Carl's words echo. *"We're made of star stuff."*

# 22

## Fat Guy in a Fat Boat

*One thing about being at sea is that you don't really get to stop.*
*Until you arrive in port, you're stuck, and conditions can always*
*worsen, the boat can always break in new ways, whether you're*
*prepared or not. Even in port, you can slip anchor, blow against*
*other anchored boats in crosswinds and currents, or run aground.*
*A boat simply does not allow for genuine rest. Its essential nature is*
*peril, held in check only through enormous effort and expense.*

—**DAVID VANN**, *A MILE DOWN: THE TRUE*
*STORY OF A DISASTROUS CAREER AT SEA*

So why would anybody in their right mind want to own a boat? Especially a sailboat? I'll tell you.

I grew up the son of a cop in the heavily industrial city of Perth Amboy, New Jersey. The town's greatest endowment was its prominent location at the confluence of the Kill Van Kull, the oily channel separating Staten

Island from New Jersey, and the Raritan River, which spills out of the Garden State's famous truck farming region into Raritan Bay and the Atlantic Ocean. Hence Perth Amboy's moniker of "Queen City of the Raritan Bay Area."

On Dad's infrequent days off from patrol duty and moonlighting as an ironworker, a favorite family pastime was to spend the afternoon at the beautifully peaceful park and boardwalk that edged the city's waterfront like the lacy hem of a pretty girl's slip.

It was there that I fell in love with the graceful sailboats that danced *en pointe* on the shimmering waters of the bay—toy ballerinas on a mirrored music box.

In the seemingly endless sunshine of a young boy's summer afternoons, I never guessed back then that there would be no boats in my life for another half century. So it's significant for me that this week, *Copy Cat*, my twenty-three-foot New England catboat, was taken from winter storage and is at her mooring off Buzzards Bay.

A catboat is not to be confused with a catamaran, the twin-hulled sail-boats most landlubbers are familiar with. Nor is it a sloop, the sleek, two-sail boat you frequently see heeled over to the point of capsizing. A catboat is a traditional working boat that was used by fishermen and lobstermen. It is low-slung, half as wide as it is long, and has only a single, large sail attached to a mast at the very front of the vessel. During the nineteenth and early twentieth century, catboats were everywhere.

"Menger Cats" are unique among the breed because his twenty-three-footer is equivalent to a twenty-seven-foot sloop. It can achieve a speedy seven knots, and it has enough headroom below decks for a six-foot-two man to stand tall.

What I did not know when I ordered my boat was that cancer would soon claim Bill Menger . . . and that I had just ordered the last Menger Cat to come off the line.

Chuck Westfall, an audio engineer who works many of Executive Media's corporate multimedia events, turned me on to catboats. Chuck explained that there's only a single sail to worry about, a hugely broad beam for almost unsinkable stability, and a big cockpit for entertaining guests. A cat was eminently easy to sail, he assured me.

"On a catboat," Chuck said laughing, "it's practically impossible to do anything that might spill your refreshing rum drink."

So I read up about catboats, and sure enough, Chuck was right. I fell in love with the looks and legends of a cat.

"You'll be the fat guy in the fat boat." He grinned when I told him I was going to buy one.

So here I am, another summer season of the "essential peril" of a boat—especially a sailboat in Buzzards Bay.

Buzzards Bay—the body of water between Cape Cod and mainland Massachusetts—got its ridiculous name from colonists who misidentified a large bird they saw near its shores. It was actually an osprey, but the irreversible naming damage had already been done.

Buzzards Bay always makes the top ten lists of "Most Challenging" bodies of US water in which to sail. In addition to brisk winds in the funnel-shaped bay, there is frequently contrary interplay between tides and winds on the uniformly shallow waters—fewer than fifty feet on average.

Still, so many recreational boaters are drawn to it—just as, from earliest times, our ancient ancestors clustered their dwelling places near bodies of water. As a species, we come from water and are so much composed of water that we instinctively regard it as our natural habitat.

In her memoir, *Paris France*, Gertrude Stein wrote:

*"Writers have two countries. The one where they belong and the one in which they live really . . . It is not real but it is really there."*

This is true for not only writers, but for sailors, too. And this is why we buy boats.

(Read about the sometimes perilous, always hilarious five-day journey Chuck and I made in sailing *Copy Cat* from the south shore of Long Island to her new home at Cape Cod . . . in my book, *Fat Guy in a Fat Boat*, available from Amazon.)

# 23

## Privacy, Pornography, Paradox

*The poorest man may in his cottage bid defiance to all the forces of the Crown. It may be frail, its roof may shake, the wind may blow through it, the storm may enter, the rain may enter—but the King of England cannot enter.*

**—WILLIAM PITT,** EARL OF CHATHAM,
BRITISH PRIME MINISTER, 1763

Thanks to the Brits, your home has been regarded for centuries not only as your castle, but also as your safest refuge.

Now, thanks to the Supreme Court, your cell phone has been deemed equally sacrosanct.

The Court in 2014 ruled unanimously that police generally need a warrant before searching the cell phone or personal electronic device of a person under arrest.

Chief Justice John Roberts conceded that the decision would make it harder for police to fight crime. But he dismissed that concern with the pithy observation that "privacy comes at a cost."

Wait a minute. I smell the odor of paradox hanging heavy in the air.

As a society, we expect and demand privacy. Yet, as a culture, we feverishly share—and follow—the most intimate details of our and one another's personal and public activities.

As of the third quarter of 2016, for example, more than 1.79 billion users spend what some would call an inordinate amount of time on Facebook—checking up on one another.

Then there's sexting—photos of what used to be called "privates" sent via social media.

A February 2014 study by security software firm McAfee reports that more than half of adults have sent or received "intimate content" on their mobile devices. Not teens. Adults, including a former New York City mayoral candidate.

New on the scene are reality television programs that broadcast as much skin as they can get away with:

- Discovery Channel's *Naked and Afraid*, a top-rated reality show
- The Learning Channel's *Buying Naked*, about real estate for nudists
- Syfy's *Naked Vegas*, about body painting
- Discovery's *Naked Castaway* and, most recently, *Dating Naked*

I was with the *New York Daily News* in the sixties when CBS Radio became our new competitor by converting to a 24/7 news format. The station's slogan was "All news, all the time." Today, as a *New York Times* TV critic pointed out, television is heading toward "All nude, all the time."

And out-and-out pornography? Revenue growth among adult and pornographic websites increased to $3.3 billion over the five-year period ending in 2015.

Author Damon Brown provides some history:

*"When the projector was invented roughly a century ago, the first movies were not of damsels in distress tied to train tracks or Charlie*

*Chaplin–style slapsticks; they were stilted porn shorts called stag films. VHS became the dominant standard for VCRs largely because Sony wouldn't allow pornographers to use Betamax; the movie industry followed porn's lead."*

Pope Francis has called ours "a culture paradoxically suffering from anonymity and at the same time obsessed with the details of other people's lives."

So here's a thought.

If the King of England could learn respect for his subjects in the eighteenth century, we in the twenty-first might consider engendering a renewed respect for the privacy of one another. We might consider mirroring the Exodus image of Moses before the burning bush by removing our sandals before the "sacred ground" of the other.

# 24

## *Fashionable or Foolish?*

Summer must be over. Autumn fashions are being shown.

As a straight guy who avidly watched *Queer Eye for the Straight Guy* on cable TV several years back, I've always needed help distinguishing between looking fashionable and looking foolish.

So I turned to my friend, John Girouard, a style guru based in Toronto and an annual visitor to Vieques. With his partner, Bruce, John publishes the exceptional *Bobo Feed* blog—architecture and design, fashion and styling, food and drink, travel and urban living—at http://bobofeed. blogspot.ca

"You could dress in Dior, Lanvin, or Armani and look foolish," John says. "Yet you could put on a simple white shirt and a great pair of jeans and be stunning.

"You need to keep in mind that what may appear foolish on the runways of the fashion capitals in any given season is often directional. You might see something totally outrageous that you'd swear no one would wear.

What happens is that by the time the garment arrives on the street you will still see some of its direction—but toned down by buyers to fit their customers," he continues.

"What shocks us now becomes standard fare in a few years. This has happened with exaggerated shoulders, platform shoes, skinny jeans—and will continue."

Nor is being fashionable an economic issue. "One could dress in couture and look foolish, yet the man or woman on the street who is proud and confident can look fabulous in thrift shop finds."

And let's kiss off the idea that fashion is the realm of the young. Proof point? Here's what *ENews* had to say about some of the getups at a recent Teen Choice Awards show:

> *"Chloë Moretz's and Jordin Sparks's printed outfits were a little too busy for our tastes. And then there was the mismatched gold-on-gold look from Katie Stevens. Hailee Steinfeld's slightly frumpy dress made us wish she'd went [sic] with something a bit more youthful."*

Says John: "Fashion isn't so much about youth and clothes as it is about style and attitude and self-assurance."

He's right. Is there anybody more elegant than an African American lady of a certain age off to Sunday morning services in a queenly hat?

Here's one such church lady quoted in *The Washington Post*:

> *"You have a certain air when you put on a hat. If you put on the whole shebang and you're satisfied, you walk different. You act different. And people treat you different."*

And this assurance from John: "One can never look foolish if one has the stature and confidence of wearing any garment . . . and most of all, the self-assurance and confidence that come with, dare we say it, *age*!"

Few embody this thought more than Ilona Royce Smithkin. At ninety-seven, she is a renowned Impressionist painter and teacher, a fashion model and a cabaret singer.

I give the last words to Ilona:

*"When you feel comfortable in your clothes, you look good. When your shoes fit right and your dress isn't too tight, you can forget about your looks and show off yourself. There's so much concentration on exterior beauty, you can wind up saying, 'I can't go to this party, I have nothing to wear.' Who the hell cares? If you're bringing yourself and you're a nice person, you're the life of the party."*

# 25

## *Adam's Curse*

We are afflicted by what's been called Adam's curse—awareness of our own mortality.

Unlike you and I, for example, dogs don't reflect upon themselves or worry that their breath is bad—even after they've just licked their nether regions. Their self-awareness is limited.

Living here in paradise, why am I entertaining these dark thoughts? Because I spent last weekend in Philadelphia, visiting my grandson, Connor, who's studying biology sciences and psychology at Drexel University. Connor has developed a keen interest in neuroscience and psychology. He'd like to someday improve the way these two fields can be applied—through research and clinical work—to medicine and spirituality.

He gave me a book to read so that I might understand his ambition about unlocking the secrets of the mind: *Consciousness*, by Christof Koch, a colleague of DNA co-discoverer Francis Crick. Now, thanks to Connor, I can't stop wondering about a subject few of us ever think about.

In reading the book, I learned that our inner world of mind, soul, and spirit is more a mystery than is the external universe. It comes down to one simple question: "How can something physical (brain matter) give rise to something nonphysical (feelings)?"

Think about this. Georges Lemaitre, who died in 1966, is the acknowledged "father of the big bang." A Belgian Catholic priest, Father Lemaître, while still a junior lecturer at the Catholic University of Leuven, proposed an expansionary theory of the universe at odds with the prevailing belief that the universe had always existed in a steady state. He asserted that the entire universe began with what he called a "cosmic egg" or "primeval atom"—a theory that Sir Fred Hoyle derisively dismissed as "the big bang." Father Lemaître also argued that not only was the universe expanding, but the speed of its expansion was accelerating. To Sir Fred's chagrin, the priest's theories have been substantively confirmed.

Yet, scientists and scholars still don't know what our inner, mental world is made of—much less understand why it exists at all.

In other words, astronomers can make statements with surety about the big bang—an event that took place 13.7 billion years ago. But the processes that make us aware of a toothache baffle us. Here's Christof Koch:

*"How the brain converts bioelectrical activity into subjective states, how photons reflected off water are magically transformed into the perception of an iridescent aquamarine mountain lake is a puzzle. The nature of the relationship between the nervous system and consciousness remains elusive and the subject of heated and interminable debates."*

The lack of any true scientific understanding of consciousness—especially when you consider the feats of science in other fields—leaves lots of questions. In fact, many philosophers, scientists, and medical experts accept the possibility that consciousness may rise from a source that is beyond the physical.

The concept of free will, for instance, has baffled scientists throughout the centuries. How is it that we humans are able to bring ideas and actions into existence from nothingness? This defies the most basic physical law—cause and effect.

Judy Bachrach, discussing her book, *Glimpsing Heaven: The Stories and Science of Life After Death*, told National Geographic:

> *"This is an area where a lot more scientific research has to be done: that the brain is possibly, and I'm emphasizing the 'possibly,' not the only area of consciousness. That even when the brain is shut down, on certain occasions consciousness endures. One of the doctors I interviewed, a cardiologist in Holland, believes that consciousness may go on forever. So the postulate among some scientists is that the brain is not the only locus of thought."*

In a world where science has pretty much tossed out nonphysical concepts from serious inquiry, paradoxes like this remain—the human capacity to "create through intention."

Where do we go from here? Perhaps:

- Continuing deep curiosity about the role of spirituality
- A profound responsibility to hone for the better the "seemingly divine" tool of conscious awareness of ourselves and of our world
- Final acceptance that each person wields wondrous power to manipulate the world in any way we please

Charles Duell was the commissioner of the US Patent Office in 1899. He is most famous because of a quote attributed to him: "Everything that can be invented has been invented."

In hindsight, we realize that if Mr. Duell did in fact utter those words, he was an ignoramus.

The lesson for me is that, just when I've reached the advanced age when I start to actually buy into the idea that I have achieved some level of "wisdom," along comes a grandchild—perhaps one I once taught to tie a shoelace—to teach me how little I really know . . . and how much more there is to learn.

# 26

## *Recess Rhythms*

There is an elementary school about a half-mile from my house in Vieques, and when the school year is in session, I can hear the distant playground sounds of the children.

Ever notice that playground noise sounds the same, whether the kids are speaking Spanish, English, or Swahili?

It brings to mind the sounds of my own childhood in Perth Amboy, New Jersey, in the fifties. Especially the rhythms and rhymes of the girls playing jump rope during recess.

Back in those fifth-grade days, I attended Shull School, a big, classically designed school set on a hill. On either side of the building were playgrounds, situated above sidewalk level. There was a playground for boys and another for girls, just as there were a boys' entry door and staircase as well as a similar arrangement for the girls.

Now, each generation of little kids believes they are the first to think up novel ways to deceive teachers. In my case, I ran with a pack of little perverts who thought we were the first to notice that all the girls wore dresses or skirts and if we casually stood on the sidewalk below the girls' playground, we could nonchalantly look up as the girls jumped rope—and treat ourselves to a peek of thigh or, if the gods were kind that day, a blur of underwear.

Skipping rope, for some reason, has always been done almost exclusively by girls. Maybe because girls are better than boys at displaying athletic poise while articulating memorized or spontaneous rhyming patterns. It could be two girls swinging the rope, for example, sometimes swinging two ropes simultaneously or even two girls in the middle, skipping in unison.

Over on the boys' playground, meanwhile, we goonies just ran around chaotically or engaged in fistfights.

Where did the tradition of skipping rope to the cadences of rhythmic rhymes come from? I haven't found any definitive answer. Girls make them up, it seems, and teach them to one another and to younger girls.

Girls and boys have their own parallel cultures and spread stories and rhymes and bits of nonsense to one another, passing them down to younger children, and forgetting them as they grow up. There's a whole world of creativity going on underneath our noses, of which we adults are largely unaware, despite having participated in it ourselves at one time.

The rhythms we hear during recess do have effect, though, and affect our point of view. One folklorist theorizes that some girls' rhymes hint at fears of puberty and the consequences of sex—in masked language:

*Cinderella, dressed in yellow,*
*Climbed the stairs*
*To kiss a fellow.*
*Kissed a snake*
*By mistake.*
*How many doctors*
*Will it take?*

Some rhymes might be nothing more than a clever way of being naughty—without rousing the ire of teachers and parents:

*Miss Annie had a steamboat*
*The steamboat had a bell*
*Miss Annie went to Heaven*
*The steamboat went to*
*Hell-o*
*Operator*
*Give me number nine*
*If you disconnect me*
*I'll kick your fat*
*Behind*
*The 'frigerator*
*There was a piece of glass*
*Mary sat upon it*
*And broke her big fat*
*As-k*
*Me no more questions*
*I'll tell you no more lies*
*Tell that to your mother*
*The day before she dies.*

One positive aspect of rhyming has been demonstrated conclusively: familiarity with rhymes is a strong foundation for reading literacy. Studies confirm that the better children are at detecting rhymes, the quicker and more successful they will be at learning to read, despite any differences in class background, general intelligence, or memory ability.

Shouldn't publishers of children's books know this kind of thing? So why did Dr. Seuss—the father of rhymed stories for children—suffer rejections by scores of publishers before his first book was printed?

# 27

## *Once Upon a Time*

I read my friend Jeffrey Alexander's book, *Obama Power*, in one rainy Sunday afternoon. It asserts that although pundits wrote off Obama as a one-term wonder after the Democratic congressional losses of 2010, he won reelection two years later by using storytelling techniques we've known since humans sat around the fire in caves.

With the State of the Union address in 2011, writes Alexander, the Lillian Chavenson Saden Professor of Sociology at Yale, Obama created a fictional character and drew a plotline that ended in, "This is what change looks like."

Opponent Mitt Romney, on the other hand, had little difficulty putting points on the board, but he had problems narrating himself heroically. Professor Alexander quotes Peggy Noonan, speechwriter for President George H. W. Bush, "Mr. Romney couldn't articulate a way forward, and nobody knew what his presidency would look like."

"It is storytelling, not policy," concludes Professor Alexander, "that defines presidential success."

Because perception can define performance, storytelling also has become corporate America's latest buzzword for everything from brand marketing to social media to employment résumés.

Persuasion is the core of commerce. Customers must be sold on a product, employees motivated to buy into a strategy, investors convinced to trust in a stock. But despite the critical importance of persuasion, most executives struggle to communicate, let alone to influence and inspire.

Robert McKee is an award-winning screenwriter and director. In a classic *Harvard Business Review* article some years ago, he was quoted as describing two ways to persuade people. The first is to use conventional rhetoric usually consisting of a PowerPoint slide presentation that builds a business executive's case via statistics and quotes from experts.

"But there are two problems with rhetoric. First, the people you're talking to have their own set of authorities, statistics, and experiences. While you're trying to persuade them, they are arguing with you in their heads. Second, if you do succeed in persuading them, you've done so only on an intellectual basis. That's not good enough, because people are not inspired to act by reason alone," McKee said.

The other way to persuade people—a more powerful way—is by uniting an idea with an emotion via a compelling story. McKee:

> *"In a story, you not only weave a lot of information into the telling but you also arouse your listener's emotions and energy. If you can harness imagination and the principles of a well-told story, then you get people rising to their feet amid thunderous applause instead of yawning and ignoring you."*

Persuasion is the centerpiece not only of business activity, but also of much human endeavor. And we've struggled forever about how to do it.

As long ago as the fourth century BC, for example, Aristotle was wondering what makes a speech persuasive. He came up with three types of appeal: ethical, emotional, and logical. A rhetorician strong on all three, he said, was likely to produce a persuaded audience.

Replace the word *rhetorician* with *politician* . . . or *executive* . . . or *brand* . . . and Aristotle's insights seem entirely modern.

# 28

## *Queen of the Fairies*

The first time I met Ilona, she lay flat on her back in her bed, beckoning me to kiss her. The only problem was that my wife was in the room.

I had come to pick up my wife, Jo Anne, after the painting class she was taking, taught by impressionist artist Ilona Royce Smithkin. Ilona had been felled by severe back pain and had taught the class from her bed in her Provincetown studio. But at ninety-four years of age, Ilona forbids her inner light to dim. She powers it with inner energy:

- Every day, she paints, swims in Cape Cod Bay and goes for walks through Provincetown—her summer home since the 1940s—or in Manhattan's West Village, where she winters.
- She teaches, accepts commissions, and does personal appearances.
- She performs her *Eyelash Cabaret* to sold-out audiences in Provincetown and Manhattan, singing throaty ballads reminiscent of Marlene Dietrich and Edith Piaf—and winning standing ovations each time she renders "La vie en rose."

"Otherwise, it's bye-bye baby," is how she justifies her energetic lifestyle.

Ilona fled Berlin with her family in 1938. Her father smuggled only enough money to tide them over until he learned English. Today—although she may not have the celebrity of other mononymous figures like Cher, Madonna, or Beyoncé—she is known to her devotees by the single name Ilona, which also happens to be the name of the queen of the fairies in Hungarian folklore.

At a recent dinner party at the Wellfleet home of Dr. Bill Shay and his partner, Jim Hood, Ilona displayed her skill as a *raconteuse*. Some samples:

- She discovered Cape Cod in 1942 or 1945—Ilona forgets which, exactly—when she asked a travel agent to recommend a place to go where, she posed, "I might meet someone or, if I don't meet someone, a place where I could at least go bike riding."

- On a romantic trip to Nova Scotia with a would-be lover: "It was the first time I saw lobster. He took me to dinner, ordered champagne, and then they brought out two steamed lobsters, amorously entwined on the platter. I said, 'How can you eat this? Their eyes are pleading with you!' I didn't eat dinner and there was no sex, either."

- But she did marry the man who took her for a date on his motorcycle. "He told me all the other girls were too afraid to ride with him on his motorcycle. After I went for a ride with him, I didn't hear from him for two weeks. When he came around again, I asked where he'd been. He said, 'I wanted to see if I could live without you. I can't.' "

Although she is a larger-than-life lady, Ilona is a petite woman—well under five feet and far less than one hundred pounds. So it could have been understandable when a visitor to a South Carolina gallery showing asked Ilona about the size of her panties. "I thought it was a rather personal question. Then I figured out that in her Southern accent, she was saying 'paintings.' "

Ilona frequently bursts into song to underline a point she wants to make. To me she likes to sing: *Peter, Peter, du war meine beste schtick.* You don't need Google Translate to figure out that one. In the same way, she continuingly jests about her advanced age, accepting that, as for all of us someday, "the darkness sets in."

Another larger-than-life lady, Rosa Parks, is attributed to have said, "Each person must live their life as a model for others."

Ilona has been just that—a model.

At the dinner table that evening at Bill and Jim's, Ilona enjoyed her companions and, between her anecdotes, reveled in regaling us with wisdom gained during ten decades:

- "Nice people find one another, like rivulets running to rivers."
- "My painting now is bolder because I don't care anymore what people say about my work."
- "I never criticize, because I'm happy to be alive."
- "I expect nothing, so whatever happens, it's a surprise."
- "I believe unendurable pleasure should be prolonged."

Dear Ms. Ilona, you find pleasure in every person and in every moment . . . and we pray you enjoy a very prolonged life.

[When this book went to press in the summer of 2017, Ilona had celebrated her ninety-seventh birthday.]

# 29

## *Cookie-Cutter People*

*In order to be irreplaceable, one must always be different.*

**—Coco Chanel**

The Town of Truro sent two of its paid flaneurs* to our house last week to appraise it for a revised tax assessment. While one of them sauntered through the rooms snapping photos, I mentioned to the other that our house might be difficult to evaluate because it is unique. He explained that house assessments are determined by an algorithm. Plug in the metrics and a computer spits out the valuation you are taxed on.

"We don't use the word 'unique' and you shouldn't either," he told me *soto voce*. "Banks don't like to finance 'unique' dwellings because of resale."

And there you have one of the significant shortcomings of our society. Homogeneity.

We hear so much about the importance of being true to yourself and of thinking outside the box. But in practice, we've become cookie-cutter people: from chain restaurants serving up taste-alike food to chain cloth-ing stores serving up look-alike fashion.

Did this ubiquitous and tedious conformity begin when we started telling every child in the school that he or she was special? Did it start when no kid left the playing field a loser?

This from Nolan Bushnell, founder of Atari—and former boss and mentor of Steve Jobs:

> *"A lot of what is wrong with corporate America has to do with a culture filled with antibodies trained to expel anything different. HR depart-ments often want cookie-cutter employees, which inevitably results in cookie-cutter solutions."*

In 1956, William H. Whyte published *The Organization Man.* It was regarded as a breakthrough sociological commentary and became a best-seller because it so courageously described what was happening on a mass scale to post-war American society: television, affordable cars, fast food. Families were nuclear, and "following your bliss" led to planned suburban communities like the tract houses ubiquitous in 1950s California.

Whyte was alarmed by this phenomenon and he wanted us to be alarmed, too. The American belief in the perfectibility of society, he wrote, was shifting from one of individual initiative to one achieved at the expense of the individual:

> *"Once upon a time it was conventional for young men to view the group life of the big corporations as one of its principal disadvantages. Today, they see it as a positive boon."*

A few years later, Richard Yates published his first novel, *Revolutionary Road,* which was nominated for the 1962 National Book Award. It illus-trated the underbelly of Ward and June Cleaver's TV family: the ideal-ized model of lifelong career, two-child family, and sensible house in the suburbs.

In the 2008 movie adaptation of *Revolutionary Road,* frustrated house-wife April Wheeler tells her husband, Frank, in a pivotal scene:

*"Our whole existence here is based on this great premise that we're special. That we're superior to the whole thing. But we're not. We're just like everyone else! We bought into the same, ridiculous delusion."*

The late British Prime Minister Margaret Thatcher used to call political correctness "fashionable consensus." And it just might be more insidious than Whyte's "group life" because it morphed into "groupthink."

Here's April Wheeler again:

*"Tell me the truth, Frank. Remember that? We used to live by it. And you know what's so good about the truth? Everyone knows what it is however long they've lived without it. No one forgets the truth, Frank, they just get better at lying."*

*Flaneur: A man who saunters around observing society

# 30

## *A Life in Black and White*

Everybody has to have an Aunt Sally in their lives. Without one, life is less.

My Aunt Sally would have been ninety-seven today if Parkinson's disease hadn't taken her in 2001.

Unlike my mother, who quit school after the eighth grade, Aunt Sally was a high school graduate. She carved a lifelong career for herself as head of Personnel for the IRS headquarters in Manhattan.

And she was such an influence on me that my mother was jealous of her.

I had inherited Aunt Sally's severe overbite, and she must have known that this malocclusion would adversely affect my self-image as it had hers. So she took me to an orthodontist while I was still in middle school and paid for braces to straighten my severely buck teeth.

She took me on an eighth-grade graduation trip to DC, encouraged me to study for the priesthood and visited me in the seminary every parents' day because my mother and father never did. When I determined that I did not have a calling to the priesthood, she steered me toward Fordham to complete my university studies.

Like the movies that were the dominant cultural centerpiece for so many people in the 1940s and 50s, she was a woman who lived her life in black and white. Decisions, choices, directions were easy, and to this day I cite Aunt Sally's many aphorisms as worthy and relevant guideposts along life's journey:

*"When you're entertaining, you never want to look chintzy"* . . .
*"Never act hoity-toity around people"* . . .
*"It's God's baby, not yours . . ."*

The "Aunt Sophie" character in my novel-in-progress, *Little Flower: A Killing on Cape Cod*, is drawn in part from my real-life Aunt Sally:

*"Jenny was sure her Aunt Sophie would hate the house. After all, she had appointed herself arbiter of what in Jenny's life was good or bad. Aunt Sophie wasn't coming to Cape Cod to eat clam rolls and lobsters, but to pass judgment on Jenny's new place. Presuming the infallibility of the Pope, Aunt Sophie proclaimed ex cathedra on the range of life's decisions—Ipana is the only toothpaste to buy; beds should be made up immediately upon rising; Milky Way candy bars are best."*

Unlike fictional Aunt Sophie, though, real Aunt Sally was a reverent woman. You would find her at early Mass every Sunday, always occupying the same pew. During her long commutes to work, she read and reread the essays of Bishop Fulton J. Sheen as if they were divinely inspired. She even had a schoolgirl's crush on her handsome pastor with the beautiful tenor voice.

After spending her prime years alone, she fell in love—at fifty-four—with a coworker. A divorcee and an irreligious Protestant, he was far from her type. But he was a Yale man, and that counted for a lot to the high school graduate that Aunt Sally was. It was not a good marriage—not the congenial relationship she had anticipated and deserved. Alone again after her husband's death from advanced alcoholism, Aunt Sally's latter years were sad ones.

French writer Simone de Beauvoir said: "One is not born, but rather becomes, a woman."

My Aunt Sally didn't know she was strong, wasn't aware she was an inspiration. She thought she was, simply, a woman.

# 31

*Learning to Learn*

*The illiterate of the 21st century will not be those who cannot read
and write, but those who cannot learn, unlearn, and relearn.*

**—ALVIN TOFFLER**

My father's ambition when he was graduated from Perth Amboy High School was to be an attorney, but it was the time of the Great Depression and he entered the workplace instead, as a laborer.

He could:

- Drive a truck
- Hang wallpaper
- Paint a house
- Repair cars
- Build furniture
- Sew slipcovers and make curtains

- Build a doghouse
- Put up a fence
- Work as an ironworker in constructing whole buildings
- Tend bar
- Pass civil service exams to become a patrolman and then a sergeant

When he had his heart attack, he was at his retirement job as a taxi dispatcher.

They used to call guys like him a "jack-of-all-trades." Today we would call him a lifelong learner.

The annual report on mortality rates by the National Center for Health Statistics, released in September 2014, confirmed that in 2012 life expectancy for older Americans continued to climb. People who reach 65 have an average 19.3 more years ahead of them—an all-time high.

What are we going to do with all this newfound time? If you're a lifelong learner—you can do plenty, because you understand that learning is not a place, but a process whose endpoint has been extended.

Learning as we used to understand it occurs in institutions designed to deliver education. The informal learning that is lifelong is most often pursued outside the walls of academic institutions.

A lot has been written about the benefits of lifelong learning: personal development, employment and earnings, economics, a sense of well-being—even as a defense against dementia. Governments are promoting lifelong learning as a way to nurture competitiveness, innovation, and growth. Some governments see lifelong learning as contributing to social cohesion.

But what about the value of a life? Does lifelong learning heighten the value of our lives?

In 2008, *Time* magazine reported that a human life was worth $189,000. In 2011, the Environmental Protection Agency set the value of human life at $9.1 million. The same year, the Food and Drug Administration put it at $7.9 million. Each of these reports crunched various numbers to come up with their assessments.

My father was deft at adding value to his life by using his hands to shape the physical environment around him. Lacking his aptitude, I've brought value to my life through my writing, and tried to add to its value through continued learning. In recent years, for example, I've learned to swim and to snorkel, to sail, to operate two well-regarded bed-and-breakfasts. I've taught myself to cook well enough to serve paying guests. I'm wrestling with Rosetta Stone to learn Italian. And I'm in the process of writing and publishing five more books.

Mary Ann Evans—the acclaimed English novelist of the Victorian era who wrote under the pen name George Eliot—said it well: "It's never too late to be what you might have been."

# 32

## *Family Candy*

*Candy corn is the only candy in the history of America that's never been advertised. And there's a reason. All of the candy corn that was ever made was made in 1911. And so, since nobody eats that stuff, every year there's a ton of it left over.*

**—LEWIS BLACK**

On my first day in kindergarten, Sister Mary Theresa passed around a big can of gumdrops for us to sample. I took two gumdrops even though she told us to each take one. The kid next to me snitched. That's when I learned never to trust anybody who doesn't like candy.

There's something about candy that defines us in a way few other things can.

Ronald Reagan, for instance, noted, "You can tell a lot about a fellow's character by his way of eating jelly beans."

When Reggie Jackson belted three home runs during Game 6 of the 1977 World Series, perhaps his greatest tribute was having a candy bar named after him.

Actor Telly Savalas built his "Kojak" character around a lollipop.

In our family, my wife's grandfather concealed a stash of Mounds bars as a special treat just for her—always, and only, Mounds. Our two daughters, on the other hand, somehow got it into their heads that their mother adored Necco Wafers. So each birthday, Mother's Day, and Christmas, Mom would be heaped with packs of the sugary disks. It wasn't until the girls were grown that she confessed to them that she hated Necco Wafers.

There is a nostalgia associated with candy. Hershey's has been around since 1900. You can find a recipe for s'mores in the *Girl Scout Handbook* of 1927. Some of us still remember the Chuckles ad slogan, "Five colors, five flavors, five cents." And three traditional favorites comprise the top-sellers every year:

- Reese's Peanut Butter Cups, introduced in 1928
- Snickers, introduced in 1930
- M&Ms, introduced in 1941

Here's Dr. Samira Kawash, an expert on the cultural history of candy, in a *Smithsonian* interview a few years ago:

*"There's no sign of trick-or-treating at all until the 1930s and it really wasn't until the late 1940s that it became widespread. . . . In the 1970s, there was the emergence of the myth of the Halloween sadist: the idea that there are people out there who are going to poison the popcorn balls, put razors in the apples, etc. Anything that wasn't factory-sealed wasn't considered safe. . . .there was a sense of loss of small-townness in that era of suburbanization. The neighbors were strangers for the first time."*

Today, though, children go from home to home trusting that strangers will give them something sweet—and safe. Adults feel no hesitation in giving candy to the small strangers on their doorstep.

At Halloween, we typically are not even cognizant of the sharing that is occurring. One poll showed that at Halloween most of us shop for the candy we favor, like a legacy we're proud to leave the kids.

In the film, *The Judge*, the title character's passion for Bit-O-Honey candies is handed down to his son, who in turn passes it down to his daughter. A powerful moment comes when the crusty patriarch is near death and his son surprises him with a handful of Bit-O-Honeys. Candy becomes a tangible metaphor for the renewed affection the two men share—despite the strained relationship they've had for years.

For this fictional family, as for my family and perhaps yours, too, a brand of humble candy can serve as a bequest whose value defies definition.

# 33

## *Psychogeography*

I am standing as far east as I can and still be in the continental United States, gazing from Truro's ocean beach across the Atlantic directly toward Spain.

It's November, the liminal month of transition from sultry summer to chill winter, from long days to long nights, from life to death. It's the month of which essayist Joseph Addison, loyal subject of the restored Stuart monarchs, said: "The gloomy month of November, when the people of England hang and drown themselves."

As I gaze at the vast gray sameness, I ask myself, "Can any place on the planet still be new?"

In mid-twentieth-century Paris, the Situationist movement attacked city planning as organized social isolation because it was concerned primarily with the smooth flow of automobile traffic.

Situationist Guy Debord called for research into the effects of urban and natural environments on emotions and behavior. He termed this area of inquiry "psychogeography." It wasn't long before his adherents adopted the practice of going on long, aimless walks—literally translated from the French *dérive* as "driftings"—to experience the psychological states and thoughts generated during their ramblings.

In 2007 British journalist Will Self wrote *Psychogeography*, which has been called a "meditation on the vexed relationship between psyche and place."

For Self, writing at a time when everything everywhere looks increasingly the same, walking is a way to see the world anew—often in striking ways.

Perhaps this is why his peregrinations took him beyond the cityscape, to the "Empty Quarters" outside urban boundaries and off paved paths. For him, these are the true frontiers, the last places left to discover and explore.

Which leads to my question, "Can any place be new?"

To try to find out, I've started to walk Cape Cod's great Outer Beach from the old Coast Guard station in Eastham to Race Point Light at Provincetown. It's the same route traveled by Henry David Thoreau in 1849.

This just might be the longest stretch of uninterrupted sand and surf in the world—twenty-five miles. On my left are sheer dunes that spike up to 140 feet and on my right 3,000 miles of deep Atlantic Ocean. "There is no other landscape like it anywhere," Robert Finch wrote in his introduction to the 1949 edition of Thoreau's *Cape Cod*.

What do I hope to accomplish with this adventure? It has to be more than tramping across twenty-five miles of geography. Will I grow, change, gain some new wisdom? Maybe it will be something as simple as falling in love with the real Cape Cod after living here for almost twenty years— just as one falls in love with a mate in a different way after many years together, when the chemistry has calmed and one finds new affection for the reality—not just the appearance.

A book will emerge from this. I already have the working title: *Chasing Thoreau*. I won't be writing so much about what I see as about what I feel. My hope is that the ideas and emotions that emerge during this long ramble will be more engaging than the act itself.

Perhaps there is another, more transcendent reason why I choose to do this in the autumn of my life, as days dwindle down. Henry Rollins, the hard-to-categorize punk legend, occasional actor, writer, and broadcast host, said it for me: "The month of November makes me feel that life is passing more quickly. In an effort to slow it down, I try to fill the hours more meaningfully."

# 34

## *Counterfeit Cancer Patient*

I am a counterfeit cancer patient. Not by choice, but by chance. And it's illuminated my idea of Thanksgiving.

As I've mentioned in some of my previous blog posts, my wife is a breast cancer survivor of fifteen years. Each month, she and I visit Memorial Sloan-Kettering Cancer Center in Manhattan for a few days of appointments, during which time we are accommodated at Hope Lodge.

Hope Lodge is a truly wonderful endeavor of the American Cancer Society—and largely run by volunteers. The ACS maintains thirty-one of these free, hotel-like accommodations in cities across the nation for patients and their caregivers who must travel long distances from home when their best hope for effective treatment is in another city. Not having to worry about where to stay or how to pay for lodging enables patients to focus on getting well.

At New York City's Hope Lodge, a significant portion of the patients are recovering from bone marrow transplants—a regimen typically lasting some hundred days, when extreme precautions must be taken to protect severely compromised immune systems.

Of course, these patients—both men and women—have lost all their hair. In addition, almost all the other patients at Hope Lodge are undergoing some measure of chemotherapy, which has stolen their hair as well.

My wife's medication is hormonal. So she still has her thick crop of blonde hair. I, on the other hand, have a shaved head.

When we meet people in the corridors or the lobby or the dining room, they invariably acknowledge us with the unvarying greeting of cancer survivors who have learned to take life one day at a time: "How is it going today?"

Except—when they ask this—they are looking at me, not my wife.

They think I'm the one with cancer.

At first I thought this was funny. Not anymore. Especially not with Thanksgiving upon us next week. In fact, I cringe when I think of how little gratitude I offer heavenward that I am not the one bound up in the struggle against the scourge of cancer.

The bald men and women at Hope Lodge who are our new friends are thankful every day. In the dining room or the lounge, it's not uncommon for them to join in applause for a fellow patient who is having a "good day," or has announced some fragment of positive news about their progress.

What is most shocking to me is that so many of these are young people:

- Tom, a bone marrow transplant patient, who left a wife and four small children when he died months after I had met him
- Maria from upstate New York, anxious about properly caring for her thirty-something husband, just out of three days in ICU after his transplant
- Chris, a Long Island metastatic breast cancer survivor herself, serving as caregiver for her husband, Michael, who is frightened about undergoing yet another facial surgery

These valiant people, and millions more who deal with cancer, are thankful for each day they prevail. For them, as it now is for me, every day is Thanksgiving Day.

# 35

## *Bic Generation*

*Made in Japan* used to mean the product was junk, until W. Edwards Deming brought his message of quality to Japanese manufacturers. We need another Deming—this time for China.

*Made in China* has become code for *cheap*—in the most negative connotation of the word:

- Appliances with a useful life of three to five years
- Napkins and tissues that shred in my hand
- Plastic bottles too thin to grip

We live in a disposable culture, where dumping something when it breaks is cheaper than fixing it.

Call it the Bic Generation, if you will, derived from the pens and lighters that started us on the road away from a fix culture to a toss culture.

Zack Whittaker writing in *ZDNet*, called it the iGeneration, with the *i* representing both the types of mobile technologies being heralded by children and adolescents (iPhone, iPod, Wii, iTunes) plus the fact that these technologies are mostly "individualized" in the way they are used.

"The iGeneration don't care about products lasting," Whittaker noted. "They just want something here and now, that will do the job and something they can dispose of without it hurting their wallets when that moment comes."

The worry, though, is not just that every *thing* is disposable in today's Bic Generation. This mentality sometimes extends to every *one*.

The University of Minnesota, for example, found that the divorce rate hasn't declined since 1980, as was thought. When the university's researchers controlled for changes in the age composition of the married population, they discovered that the divorce rate actually rose by 40 percent.

In reporting the story, *The Washington Post* wrote: "The flipside of this finding is the relative rarity of divorce among younger Americans today. In the 1970s, a couple might get married at twenty-five and be divorced by thirty. But today, that same couple would be more likely to simply live together for a few years and then head their separate ways when things go south."

"When things go south." It can apply to our children, too.

In a November 2014 report, the National Center on Family Homelessness found that the number of homeless children in the United States had surged to an all-time high—nearly 2.5 million children homeless at some point in 2013. That's one child in every thirty.

The blame? The center pointed to our high poverty rate, the lack of affordable housing, and the impacts of pervasive domestic violence.

But I wonder how many of these young people were thrown out of the house because they were considered "broken"—gay, lesbian, bisexual, transgender, or pregnant?

An independent film titled *The Disposable Generation*, sought to capture the writer/director's view that today "numbness is a virtue . . . an apathetic youth favors the modern American Dream, which doesn't necessarily involve being awake anymore."

There might be hope. A recent Twitter exchange that I saw went like this:

The post: *We're the "everything is disposable" generation. We dont like it we replace it. If its broke we throw it out. If its too hard we quit on it*

The reply: *Not quite. Dnt like it? We make it better. Broke? Make it so it doesnt break again. Too hard? Make it easier.*

# 36

## *All Talk*

Vieques might be a tropical paradise, but it's no Garden of Eden. The Viequense diet favors meats, plantains, rice, and beans. Not much in the way of fruit or vegetables is grown here. Instead, most is imported—and refrigerated during transportation. As a result, bananas slip off the stalk, peaches segue directly from unripe to rotten, and tomatoes are disappointingly pink, mealy, and tasteless.

A resourceful Puerto Rican fellow brings a truckload of produce from the main island of Puerto Rico two or three days a week—if the cargo ferries are running right. He parks on the shoulder of the road outside the General Electric manufacturing plant, sets up tables under a tent and serves as our green grocer. Expat North American residents, restaurant chefs, and even tourists make it a routine to shop there.

When I built a house in Vieques a few years ago, I quickly discovered that Puerto Rican Spanish is different from what's spoken in Spain and Latin and Central America. Viequense Spanish is yet another step toward the incomprehensible. The locals speak very rapidly. They drop all the *esses* and pronounce as *j* the "y" in *yo* and the double *l*'s in, say, *calle*. In addition, they employ a host of island-specific slang. For example, *wha-wha* for an SUV type of vehicle—which sounds to me like baby talk. I have, in fact, given up my original ambition to learn Spanish.

With my minimal Spanish, I have to concentrate hard on numbers beyond ten. So it's a struggle for me to understand how much money to hand over for my weekly basket of fruits and vegetables. When I spent a month in Florence, on the other hand, I found that the mellifluous words of the Italian language practically "stuck" to my brain. Within a week or two, I was starting to get by in basic conversational Italian.

Research by Jean Berko Gleason, the psycholinguist, shows speech discernment not only begins in the womb, but also affects the development of the fetal brain. The brain of a fetus in a bilingual environment tends to develop a disposition toward bilingual speech.

This leads me to thank my mother for yet another gift—in addition to life itself. While she was pregnant with me, she lived in a household where both English and Ukrainian were spoken. In my formative years I spoke both, but English predominated and I never became fully fluent in Ukrainian.

But I do have what Gleason called a "disposition toward bilingual speech." I have a command of conversational Ukrainian. In high school I studied German. At Fordham University, I minored in Latin and Greek. I know a bit of Spanish, as I mentioned, and I'm trying to learn Italian. At my Manhattan apartment, there were mornings when I'd pass through the lobby and greet the security guy in Russian, wish the custodian a good day in Spanish and ask the Brazilian doorman if *todo bem* today.

This makes me agree with researchers who claim, "If we used a different vocabulary or if we spoke a different language, we would perceive a somewhat different world."

The pity is that the only language I am truly comfortable in is English. I blame myself for not being smart enough or studious enough to be fully bilingual. But maybe I shouldn't be so hard on myself. After all, it was

Maria Montessori, the brilliant educator, who found that, "There is . . . in every child a painstaking teacher, so skillful that he obtains identical results in all children in all parts of the world. The only language men ever speak perfectly is the one they learn in babyhood, when no one can teach them anything!"

# 37

## *Nothing On*

She's fifty-one inches of ebony glamour corner to diagonal corner—as glistening and glassy smooth as a wet crow's wing. Sexy, seductive, high-maintenance, classy, and trashy all at once.

She's my new Samsung F8500 Smart plasma television set with Evolution Port, Quad Core Processor, and 600 Hz Subfield Motion. I don't even need a remote control—I can use hand gestures to change channels. And *TV Guide*, which was once the largest-circulation magazine? Forget about it! I simply ask my Samsung F8500 and she will respond to my voice with a selection of programs based on my preferences.

Loren Cuming, the twenty-something son of our architect, pimped the Samsung F8500. He said this was what we had to have as part of his mom's renovation of our Cape Cod house. Nothing else comes close for true black color.

True black color? Yes, that's what he said. Other TVs can't provide true black—only very dark grays. Oh, and it's not a TV set. It's a flat screen.

But why did we ever listen to this technology know-it-all? Who needs all this electronic, plasmatic firepower to stare at the twaddle put out by television programmers?

As author Jarod Kintz said, "A window is more entertaining than TV. Just ask a cat looking out . . ."

Here's what my wife and I watch, the complete list: *Chopped*, *Love It or List It*, *Judge Judy*, and almost anything on TCM.

To see a movie on TCM that was filmed in black and white seventy-five years ago, we need a TV that sells for $2,376.21?

That price was just for starters.

The custom-built shelving and cabinetry to house our black beauty was $6,500.

She comes with a hunk of steel to mount her to the wall. But the articulating arm to enable tilting and swiveling listed at $150.

Despite shelling out $2,376.21, we were advised by the Best Buy salesman that the Samsung's audio quality really isn't up to snuff. So he sold us a really cool sound bar for $229.

Installation by two Geek Squad techs, including extra-long cabling to the new Blu-ray player, added $441.

The final insult was learning that we needed a high-def receiver. To get one from DIRECTV, we had to renew our contract for two years and pay an additional $10 a month for the new box.

All this money for what once was free.

I spent most of my life in the New York City metropolitan region served by the three networks and a clutch of local channels. So what if our old DuMonts and Admirals and Philcos were victim to intermittent vertical roll, snow, and ghost images? So what if we had to actually get up from the couch to change channels or fiddle with rabbit ears? TV was free and I could always find something to watch. Today, with access to hundreds of channels, I usually find, "There's nothing on."

As W. H. Auden wrote, "What the mass media offers is not popular art, but entertainment which is intended to be consumed like food, forgotten, and replaced by a new dish."

# 38

## *A Few of My Most-Hated Things*

Distill into a single flask all the synthetic sweetness and faux sentimentality of the Christmas season and *voilà*! The cloying genie in your bottle is none other than Julie Andrews.

We all have our private list of activities, things, and people we hate for no intelligible reason.

My wife hates white chocolate.

My daughter, Wendy, hates humidity.

My daughter, Julie, hates the Food Network's "Sandwich King."

And Julie Andrews singing about a few of her favorite things—I hate that. When did it become a Christmas song?

"My Favorite Things" is one of several hit songs that came out of the 1959 Rodgers and Hammerstein score of *The Sound of Music*. The song has been recorded by vocalists from Barbra Streisand and Kelly Clarkson to the cast of *Glee*.

Here's the classic version of the lyrics:

*Raindrops on roses and whiskers on kittens,*
*Bright copper kettles and warm woolen mittens,*
*Brown paper packages tied up with strings,*
*These are a few of my favorite things.*

*Cream-colored ponies and crisp apple strudels,*
*Doorbells and sleigh bells and schnitzel with noodles,*
*Wild geese that fly with the moon on their wings,*
*These are a few of my favorite things.*

*Girls in white dresses with blue satin sashes,*
*Snowflakes that stay on my nose and eyelashes,*
*Silver white winters that melt into springs,*
*These are a few of my favorite things.*

*When the dog bites,*
*When the bee stings,*
*When I'm feeling sad,*
*I simply remember my favorite things*
*And then I don't feel so bad.*

And here's my take on it:

*Flip-flops on women and cell phones on sidewalks*
*Valley Girl accents and models like beanstalks*
*Britney and Miley, who twerks when she sings,*
*These are a few of my most-hated things.*

*Beyoncé and Bieber and all the Kardashians,*
*Pelosi and Boehner and half-baked Alaskans,*
*Gluten-free muffins and Buffalo wings,*
*These are a few of my most-hated things.*

*Anchors on TV who come across clueless,*
*Talk shows with chatter that's totally mindless,*
*Half-witted athletes with pay like they're kings,*

*These are a few of my most hated things.*

*When the dog bites,*
*When the bee stings,*
*When I'm feeling sad,*
*I simply remember my most-hated things*
*And then I don't feel so bad.*

The truth of the matter is that too many of us tend to hate some part of ourselves, too. And there's the sin. Because when we unreasonably fault ourselves, we deny that we are loveable, and loved.

I'd go so far as to suggest that the opposite of hate is not love, but hope. Hope in our innate potential for goodness. Hope that the image and likeness of the Divine dwells within us. And hope in the truth of what we accept and celebrate at Christmas: "God so loved the world that he gave his only Son."

# 39

## *Voluntary Madness*

*My side felt a lot better when Nora called me at noon the next day.*
*"My nice policeman wants to see you," she said. "How do you feel?"*
*"Terrible. I must've gone to bed sober."*

**—DASHIELL HAMMETT,** THE THIN MAN

Tonight, New Year's Eve, is the high holy day of what Seneca, the Stoic philosopher of ancient Rome, called "nothing but voluntary madness."

Here on Outer Cape Cod, night has come cold and clear. Skies are star-pocked. The prevailing westerly winds are pushing twenty knots. But bars and restaurants are aglow with Christmas lights as patrons get their own alcoholic glow on.

It's the time of *auld lang syne*—old times' sake, the phrase popularized by a 1788 Robert Burns song.

Tonight I'm remembering a stellar journalist named Howard Alexander, who was my managing editor at *The Evening News* in Central New Jersey when I was a cub reporter.

Howard was the archetype of the classic newspaperman: a small, skinny man with a shock of wiry white hair, nicotine-yellowed teeth and fingers, and his daily attire of rumpled suit, wrinkled white shirt, and bowtie.

In addition to his duties as managing editor, Howard indulged himself from time to time in penning an op-ed piece when a topic intrigued him.

One of those pieces—which ran in the paper one New Year's—was a catalog of synonyms for "drunk." What made Howard's column memorable to me was that he did not use a thesaurus. He summoned up from his mind and his memory scores of different words denoting "drunk."

In fact, I don't recall ever seeing a thesaurus in the City Room of either *The Evening News* or *The New York Daily News*, where I also worked. Nor did I ever observe a reporter, rewrite man or editor at either of those newspapers refer to a thesaurus—including me.

The idea of enumerating synonyms for "drunk" was not new with Howard:

- A list of 220 expressions for *inebriated* was published by Benjamin Franklin as the "Drinker's Dictionary" in the *Pennsylvania Gazette* on January 6, 1737.
- Some 166 synonyms for *drunk* were published in the *St. Louis Republic* on June 30, 1901.
- *Roget's International Thesaurus* (which was first published in 1852 and has never been out of print) offers at least 120 synonyms for *intoxicated*.

Drinking enjoys unearned glamour—accepted, approved, encouraged. In *The Thin Man* movie franchise, for example, both Nick and Nora Charles never ventured too far without martini or highball in hand.

In my days as a reporter, for example, drinking and holding my liquor was requisite. I haunted the bars near city hall to pick up story leads from buzzed municipal officials. Then I returned to the City Room to write them—with a big container of black coffee to keep me honest.

I wasn't alone in this. The three-martini lunch popularized by 1950s "Mad Men" was real. For my newspaper crowd, though, scotch was the preferred drink, with a bottle stowed in almost every City Room desk drawer.

Philosopher Friedrich Nietzsche, who made nihilism infamous by helping shape and define it, added to the romanticizing of alcohol when he said, "For art to exist, for any sort of aesthetic activity or perception to exist, a certain physiological precondition is indispensable: intoxication."

But the romance of drinking loses its ersatz gloss with the horrid consequences of alcohol over-indulgence.

In 2014 the National Institute on Alcohol Abuse and Alcoholism reported:

- Nearly 88,000 people (approximately 62,000 men and 26,000 women) die from alcohol-related causes every year, making it the third-leading preventable cause of death in the United States.
- In 2012, alcohol-impaired-driving fatalities accounted for 10,322 deaths, or 31 percent of all driving fatalities.

Statistics become sorrows when they strike at your heart. My son-in-law, Davin, returning home from a Sunday evening date-night movie with my daughter, died after a head-on collision with a drunk driver. The other driver left her four children orphaned—and my daughter a widow at twenty-eight.

Tonight, as my wife and I count down to midnight, we will recall the people who passed through our lives during the years and left us enriched by the memory of them. Howard. And Davin. And many, many others. We will celebrate them with a prayer. Not with a toast.

# 40

*Victoria's Sleazy Secret*

Just before Christmas my little island of Vieques was all a-twitter because a gaggle of Victoria's Secret models flew in for a fashion shoot. The fuss reminded me about something most people don't know about Victoria's Secret.

The bra behemoth made the calculated decision in mid-2013 to refuse to make a line for women who have undergone mastectomy surgery.

What do we make of a corporation that trades on the breasts of women, but turns its back on those same women when those same breasts are taken by cancer?

Breast cancer does not spare younger women, either. I personally know two women who were diagnosed with breast cancer in their thirties and had radical mastectomies. Debbie Barrett, who led the effort to convince Victoria's Secret to design a "Survivor" bra, was diagnosed with breast cancer at thirty-six.

I accompany my wife, a breast cancer survivor, to her monthly treatments at Memorial Sloan-Kettering Cancer Center in New York City. On the second floor of the East Sixty-Sixth Street facility is a huge waiting room filled with scores of women of all ages, nationalities, and races. These women are there to see their oncologists. Up on the third floor is an equally large room filled with women waiting for their chemotherapy infusions.

This is only one day at one medical facility in one city. I can't guess the number of other breast cancer treatment facilities like it across the country and around the world.

An estimated 232,670 women were diagnosed with breast cancer in the United States in 2014 and 40,000 died.

I know a little about how product development and marketing decisions are made. The process starts with defining market requirements—in other words, can we sell enough units to make the profit we want?

But that's not the way Victoria's Secret explained their decision:

*"Through our research, we have learned that fitting and selling mastectomy bras in the right way, a way that is beneficial to women, is complicated and truly a science. As a result, we believe that the best way for us to make an impact for our customers is to continue funding cancer research."*

There is a facet of a company's character called corporate citizenship. It encompasses things like support of the arts, respecting the environment, contributing to research and charitable programs. Call it "doing the right thing."

Here's Sheila Moeschen, writing in *Huffington Post* about the ill-considered corporate citizenship of Victoria's Secret:

*"A woman living as a cancer survivor is not just a body transformed, hers is a life transformed. Victoria's Secret could have been a part of this process. They had the opportunity to participate in the journeys of these women in meaningful ways and to make a clear and inspired statement about valuing all types of bodies, about acknowledging the*

*hidden impacts of breast cancer, and about setting an example for young women that defies the stigma associated with disease. Instead, they opted to stick to making gauzy Barbie doll peignoir sets and cotton candy-colored training bras for its 'bright young things.' "*

Victoria's Secret released its craftily worded press statement and moved on. They knew the negative publicity would subside. They knew their sleazy secret would be forgotten.

Don't let it.

# 41

## *Operator, I've Been Disconnected*

They do it in public. They do it in restaurants, right at the table. They do it on the street, in their cars. Even at the beach. You see them doing it everywhere—the solitary sin of texting.

In these early years of the twenty-first century, we've labeled ourselves the "connected society." But aren't we really more disconnected than ever? Aren't we really the "anonymous society?"

Here's just one example. At my Vieques home I had a video surveillance system installed a year ago. The cameras never worked to my satisfaction. After wading through the lengthy menu of options from the company's automated voice system, I finally got an agent on the phone and told her I wanted to cancel my account. She said I had to write a letter requesting cancellation. A written, snail-mailed letter was required when important business of all kinds is done electronically? She blandly informed me that unless I wrote a letter, the service would never be canceled and I would be billed monthly—forever.

Yet, she couldn't give me a name I could send the letter to. "Address it to the Customer Service Team," she told me.

"The team." Every communication I receive from every company now comes from "the team." A client once introduced me to her boss as "my coach."

I once worked for ROLM, the Silicon Valley company behind voice mail. They marketed their product as PhoneMail. As with so much new technology, a pristine concept was misused in the marketplace. Instead of becoming a wonderful productivity tool, voice mail became a widespread device for companies to cut headcount while ducking pesky customer conversations.

Gone is the joy of phoning a company and hearing—instead of a robotic voice—a human answering on the first ring and asking, "May I help you?"

When he was CEO of Siemens Rolm Communications, Inc., Karl Geng used to remind us that if telephones were invented just today, people would think it a miracle to conduct a real-time voice conversation.

I like something that inventor Nikola Tesla is quoted as saying after a career during which he won nearly 300 worldwide patents: "There is a difference between progress and technology. Progress benefits mankind. Technology does not necessarily do that."

# 42

## *Saints and Poets, Maybe*

The Delaware Indians called it "Town of Sandflies." It lies almost one hundred miles outside present-day Pittsburgh. Thanks to a small-town newspaper editor with not much else to print on a dreary February day in 1886, the entire United States celebrates the obscure town of Punxsutawney, Pennsylvania.

"A thousand people freezing their butts off waiting to worship a rat," Bill Murray says in the movie, *Groundhog Day*, which solidified the actor as a household name. "What a hype."

It may well be hype, but thousands of tourists pour into the town every year to see firsthand if a shadow is cast by the star of the show—a ground-hog called "Punxsutawney Phil, Seer of Seers, Sage of Sages, Prognosticator of Prognosticators, and Weather Prophet Extraordinary."

When Germans settled the area in the 1700s, they brought a tradition known as Candlemas Day. It came at the midpoint between the winter solstice and the spring equinox, when people welcomed a break from the winter routine. Clergy blessed candles and distributed them in the drear of winter. Superstition held that if the weather was fair that day, the second half of winter would be stormy and cold.

Celebration of Groundhog Day began on February 2, 1886, with a proclamation in *The Punxsutawney Spirit* by the newspaper's editor: *Today is groundhog day and up to the time of going to press the beast has not seen its shadow.*

Since then the beast and his progeny have cast a shadow 120 times—promising more winter weather—and failed only eighteen times.

In the movie, Murray portrays a character trapped in a time loop in which he repeats the same day over and over. He happens to be in Punxsutawney and it happens to be Groundhog Day.

Why is this movie a classic? Maybe it has a ring of truth we can relate to.

For many of us, doesn't life seem to be one long Groundhog Day? We trudge through stultifying daily routines, entangled in repeating patterns of resolutions forgotten, diets abandoned, disagreements rehashed.

Yet, what about Emily, the young girl in Thornton Wilder's *Our Town* who's taken from life too early? When she's offered the chance to return to Earth for one day, she is advised: "Choose the least important day in your life. It will be important enough." Sure enough, she sees that any day is an important one:

*EMILY: "Do any human beings ever realize life while they live it?—every, every minute?"*

*STAGE MANAGER: "No." Pause. "The saints and poets, maybe—they do some."*

Essayist Ken Sanes interprets *Groundhog Day* as an exceptional work of moral fiction whose Scrooge-like protagonist is exiled from normal life so he can discover the good in himself. The movie appears to express an essential truth, Sanes says. When we get beyond denial and resentment over the conditions of life and death and accept our situation, we can become authentic and compassionate.

Toward the end of the movie, Murray's character gives a speech: "Standing here among the people of Punxsutawney and basking in the warmth of their hearths and hearts, I couldn't imagine a better fate than a long and lustrous winter."

Given the wintertime beauty of my surroundings on Cape Cod, I have to agree. I can't imagine a better fate than a long and lustrous winter here.

# 43

## *Simon Says*

His name was Bill Farrell, a dashing fashion photographer in New York City who played to the hilt his role as a dashing fashion photographer. I was a young advertising rep for IBM, cutting my teeth on photo shoots of pretty models portraying computer users.

"You can tell what a woman's thighs look like by her upper arms," Bill one day informed me. "They're mirror images."

Ever since, I have gone through life burdened with the unwanted faculty of looking at a woman's bare arms, but seeing her thighs. Kind of a deviant variant of Superman's X-ray vision.

Maybe this is why I'm getting so exasperated at the barrage of photos—especially on Facebook—of young women posing for the camera with one or both hands on their hips. Akimbo.

Today's young women pose for a group photo, and each places hands on hips. I've seen wedding pictures in which all the bridesmaids—even the bride in flowing white—have hands on hips. A truly ludicrous look.

I'm told by my daughters, "Girls do that so their arms won't look fat." Who sent out the memo?

I can think of only one person with that kind of clout—Simon. The same Simon from the game we learn as children, in which the players heed only the leader's commands that start with the words "Simon says." A player who follows a command not preceded by "Simon says" is out. The object for the player acting as Simon is to get all the other players out as quickly as possible. The winner of the game is the last player who has followed the commands correctly.

Who is Simon? The name "Simon" has been attributed to the persuasive Roman orator, Cicero. Others trace it back to the thirteenth century, when Simon de Montfort captured King Henry III. Any order by Henry could be countermanded by de Montfort. Or perhaps "Simon Says" was chosen simply because kids like alliteration.

In the United States, we call the leader of this game Simon. In France, he's Jacques. In Ireland, it's O'Grady doing the saying. In Norway, "the King commands" and in Finland, "the Captain commands."

Whatever the history or the culture or the language, the point is the same: listen carefully and do exactly as "he" says.

And today's young ladies do. From summertime, when every young thing in Manhattan went to the office in flip-flops, to this year's legging-clad bottoms, this generation's adherence to conformity is breathtaking. Not only the women. Guys have their ears cocked for whatever Simon says, too. Backward caps, scruffy beards, short pants in winter.

Rachel Roy, the iconic fashion designer known for her unique style and striking, feminine pieces, could not have put it more bluntly in *InStyle* magazine in 2011: "Stop putting your hand on your hip when you take pictures!"

So why don't the young ladies listen to her? Perhaps if Rachel changed her name to Simon.

# 44

## *They Take So Much with Them*

I'm finally reading Marilynne Robinson's Pulitzer-winning novel, *Gilead*. I was stopped cold by one simple thought: that when loved ones die, they take so much with them.

That's all she says. She leaves it to you and me to summon up our own memories of deceased loved ones—of their affection toward us, their touch, their smile. All of it gone in a tremulous final breath.

Death is the signal moment in the life of a human being, when we are most aware of the loved one's uniqueness, beyond romantic love and its physical expression.

At the birth of a loved one, we are aware that something has come into being that never was before and, at their death, we are aware that something has passed away that never will be again.

What is this something that passes away with the death of a loved one? A relationship that provided us with a sense of home.

This is easy to see in children. For a child, home is not a place, but a relationship of love and trust. A child can change addresses many times and call each one home because the parents are there. As you and I mature, we form new family relationships of love and trust and, therefore, a renewed sense of home.

All definitions of love—as far back as the ancient Greek word for unselfish love, *agape*—center on the idea that we *prefer* what's best for our beloved.

Henri Nouwen, the author of many books on the spiritual life, writes: "It is exactly in the preciousness of the individual person that the eternal love of God is refracted and becomes the basis of a community of love."

Nowhere, I think, is such a "community of love" more real than in the family relationships that have such intense importance to us.

Having a home is not simply having a house. It is being tied to loved ones who care about our well-being and give us a sense of belonging—of being home.

This is why the death of a loved one is devastating. They take so much with them. They take "home."

# 45

## *C-Level Lessons of* Downton Abbey

The aristocracy featured in the popular *Downton Abbey* television series might think they wrote the book on living the pampered life. But I've worked with many C-level executives who thought themselves just as titled—and entitled.

From them I learned a few lessons on the deportment of executives once they've achieved the seeming paradise of C-level corporate aristocracy.

The fifth season of the TV series ends tomorrow. As I watched its story unfold each week, I've been struck by the similarities between the depiction of this dying breed of British upper crust and some of the corporations I've been associated with.

Just as the ladies of Downton have no interest in learning to cook and the gentlemen do not toil at a livelihood, corporate aristocracy is not expected to do anything hands-on. Downton folk write letters, visit, have tea. C-people fill their days with meetings, business meals, and travel.

Most important is to keep top of mind that C-levels are persons of privilege. Just as Downtown maids are paid to pour tea, C-levels have people paid to keep them similarly pleased. Here are some examples from my own days of corporate "service."

Whenever one CEO's wife decided to host a luncheon for the wives of her husband's colleagues or constituents, it was I who had to write the formal, flowery letters of invitation she liked.

On the first morning of a five-day, five-city road show, the CEO complained to me that the strawberries the hotel served at breakfast were not sliced. It was I who called ahead to ensure he would find correctly sliced strawberries at the next four stops.

On another occasion, the hotel where our meeting was held had a new tower under construction. The CEO had brought his wife along and the noise was bothersome to her. It was I who called the hotel's general manager to cajole him into halting construction until the lord and his lady checked out.

Newbies to corporate aristocracy learn the ropes fast:

- To have their staff inspect their suite before arrival and have their favorite refreshments waiting
- To enjoy a car and driver to convey them to and from the office each day
- To throw dinners and cocktail parties, all charged to the company

It's not a matter of thinking themselves too big for their britches. Their minions and underlings would expect no less of them.

Carson, the starched butler of *Downton Abbey*, has as a primary responsibility the duty of "ringing the gong" each evening. At its brassy sound, the ladies and gentlemen of the Abbey—and the lord, too—retire to their quarters to don formal dress for dinner. It is Carson's moment. He has control. The aristocracy steps to his summons, and steps lively.

I identify with Carson. Because in the end, it was I—and others like me who occupy staff positions such as chief of staff, director of communications, executive assistant—who operated the behind-the-scenes levers that caused the main players to act and react.

Yet, when it's all said and done, I have to be honest and agree with Downton's Lord Robert when he says, "By God I envy them, though . . . and their ability to sleep at night."

# 46

## *The Hunt for Happiness*

Life's temptations haven't changed a wit since Adam and Eve in the Garden of Eden, Christ in the desert, or Seneca in hedonistic Rome. We are lured by any proffer of sensual pleasure, exert any effort to gain the trappings of power and control, and suffer no insult to our own vain pride. Succeed in these, we believe, and we've found paradise.

Yet four of five people say they're unhappy with their very purpose in life.

After more than two million interviews during six years, this was a finding of an international Gallup-Healthways study released in September 2014.

Only 18 percent reported liking what they do each day. Put another way, most of us have little reason to get out of bed in the morning.

That's a sad thought to entertain as we set our clocks forward tonight in anticipation of the happy season of spring. But the idea that happiness is "out there" to be hunted down and possessed like the Holy Grail stretches back to Eden:

*But the serpent said to the woman: "You certainly will not die! No, God knows well that the moment you eat of it your eyes will be opened and you will be like gods who know what is good and what is bad."*

Essayist Robert Barron, in reflecting on the biblical account of Christ's three temptations in the desert, says we face these same classic enticements today:

- We place sensual pleasure at the center of our concerns, with eating, drinking, and sex paramount in our lives. Christ felt the full weight of fasting for forty days in preparation for his public ministry.
- Second, power over others is of the essence, from political dictators to control freaks within families and friendships. This was the temptation Christ faced when he was offered rule over the kingdoms of the world.
- Finally, we seek to enhance our reputation, be admired and esteemed. This was the temptation Christ fought when he was taken to the parapet of the Temple, the place of supreme visibility.

Christ's advice for the good life? "Learn from me, for I am meek and humble, and you will find rest for yourselves."

A leading light of the pagan Roman Empire, who happened to be a contemporary of Christ, also had a lot to say about the lusty appetites we humans have for pleasure, power, and pride. His name was Lucius Annaeus Seneca. As a college freshman, I spent a year translating this Stoic philosopher's writings from the Latin.

A waste of my time?

Not to *The New Yorker* magazine, which last month ran a long piece on Stoicism:

*Seneca consistently maintains that the key to a virtuous life is freedom from passion. Virtue, in turn, is necessary for happiness and also sufficient to produce it . . . the tradition placed great emphasis on austerity and self-mastery.*

Tim Ferriss, author of *The 4-Hour Workweek*, advises corporate executives to apply Stoicism as a counterweight to their entrepreneurial endeavors because it teaches how to be steadfast, strong, and in control—of yourself.

As Seneca wrote: "Show me a man who isn't a slave. One is a slave to sex, another to money, another to ambition; all are slaves to hope or fear. And there is no state of slavery more disgraceful than one that is self-imposed." He added, "It is not the man who has too little, but the man who craves more, that is poor."

Seneca laid the foundation of our understanding of free will. It is in our power to become virtuous, he said, because we decide—through reason, not emotion—how to live.

He hammers home the core note of Stoicism—that virtue alone creates happiness, and nothing else even makes a contribution.

And in saying that only virtue is good, he defines the good as something that benefits others as well as us. In fact, Seneca devotes an entire treatise, *Epistulae Morales,* to the idea:

*No one can lead a happy life if he thinks only of himself and turns everything to his own purposes. You should live for the other person if you wish to live for yourself.*

No, freedom is not found in unrestricted autonomy nor does the happy life blossom in unfettered indulgence in pleasure, power and pride.

It's closer to what Mark Twain had in mind when he said, "Live so that when we die even the undertaker will be sorry."

# 47

## *It's All About Me*

I made my daughters cry. I made my grandsons laugh. All in a day's work. That's what I did to my family with the publication of my first print book, which chronicles the calamities that can befall a Sunday afternoon sailor.

*Fat Guy in a Fat Boat* came off press a few weeks ago. One of my daughters burst into tears when her copy arrived in the mail from Amazon. The other daughter said she bawled her eyes out. But two of my grandsons recited portions to each other and laughed themselves silly at my nautical klutziness.

Publishing a book—not an eBook, but a printed book that you can hold in your hands—is the proverbial roller-coaster ride.

There is the book signing, with people *thanking* me for allowing them to buy a copy. I held my first one last Saturday at the annual meeting of the Catboat Association in Connecticut's historic Mystic seaport.

Then comes the joy of gratefully presenting a copy to the close friends who encouraged me for years.

Finally, the days on end when no sales are reported—and the nagging necessity to get on with developing the next book.

The catboat is the quintessential American working boat. Unlike the recreational sloops you see everywhere today, catboats have only one sail and a cockpit big enough for lobster traps and fishing nets. These sailboats were developed probably on Cape Cod two centuries ago and were ubiquitous until World War II.

I bought mine several years ago, christened her *Copy Cat* and have ever since been trying to learn to sail this beautiful vessel as she deserves. My misadventures reached the point where I had to write a book.

During the past week I've signed and sold a bunch of books and received congratulations and well wishes from scores of people—many of whom I've never even met.

More important, the experience has prompted me to appreciate what Amazon has demonstrated in recent years. That each of us has something to say, each of us can publish. Because we're people, and people are interesting.

As a panelist at a writing seminar, I told the attendees not to be overwhelmed by the blank page (or the blinking computer screen). Just start writing. Words will come. Rewrite later.

It was advice I wish I had followed when I was still in school. The experts told me to write every day. But I didn't. I had fallen victim to the twisted maxim, *Dying is easy; writing is hard.* So I wrote only when I was paid to.

Today I write in order to give others a glimpse into a world that only I see, because I am the one who's living it. I write a weekly blog, have two nonfiction books published, two novels with editors, and another nonfiction in progress.

The eighteenth century British literary lion Samuel Johnson is remembered not so much for his own writing as for the biography written of him by his friend, James Boswell. It's been called the greatest biography in the English language.

Few of us, if any, have a Boswell to follow us around and preserve our doings for posterity. It's our lot in life, and our opportunity, to be our own Boswell, observing and recording ourselves—if not for posterity, at least for our grandchildren.

If nothing else, they'll have a good laugh someday.

# 48

## *". . . Is Good News"*

It used to be just booze and dope. Then they added sex, porn, and food to the list of addictions that prey on us.

How about news?

Can incessant hunger for breaking news qualify as an addiction?

While I was a student at Fordham, I was lucky enough to be hired as a copy boy at the *New York Daily News*. This was when the *Daily News* was a crusading, well-written hallmark of journalism, not the throwaway tabloid it is today.

Working at the *Daily News* not only paid my way through college, but it also caused me to fall head-over-heels in love with the idea of ferreting out the truth and delivering it to readers—all for a dime.

So I cast aside my original ambition to get a PhD and teach English literature to college students. Instead, I reinvented myself as an underpaid but hard-drinking, sleeves-rolled-up, staccato–style New York City reporter.

That lasted only until I married, we had our first baby, and I went to work writing fluff for IBM so I could earn enough money to support a family.

But the newshound refused to die. It lives still, sniffing at my heels day and night. Has this caused headaches? Ask my wife. News on TV, news on the car radio, earbuds as I fall asleep to all-news radio. And the Internet? OMG . . . the Internet!

I've resolved finally to sink a wooden stake into the heart of the blood-sucking monster and give up news once and for all. Cold turkey. The way I rid myself of nicotine thirty years ago.

I have begun by giving up news for Lent. Forty days without knowing wassup.

No more *New York Times* . . . *Daily Beast* . . . Google News . . . *Wall Street Journal* . . . CNN . . . Jim Lehrer . . . AP wire . . . I could go on.

Instead of local TV news at five o'clock each evening, I enjoy my martini with Dick Van Dyke reruns.

With three weeks of Lent behind me, how is it working out? Worse than giving up smoking.

I didn't realize that without chasing news, news keeps coming at me. News items crop up everywhere on Facebook and LinkedIn. My wife mentions news items. I receive e-mails that talk about things happening in the news.

Temptation assaults me. No sooner did I drop my subscription to *The New York Times* than they e-mailed me an offer of 50 percent off an entire year's rate. How do you pass up a deal like that?

And eating alone? Without reading news? You've got to be kidding.

A confession. On two occasions I sneaked a look at Google News on my iPhone when my wife was in another room. *I had to know*!

My last resort in fighting off the temptation and hobble through until Easter is to go on retreat at the Trappist monastery in the hills of western Massachusetts. For a week, I know I will be shielded—no Internet, radio, or television. No magazines or newspapers. No conversation.

# 49

## *Robots 1, Humans 0*

I completed my retreat at the Trappist monastery. After this week without Internet, phone, television, radio, or news media, I've come to believe we humans may have already lost the robot wars hypothesized by science fiction writers.

Just as ancient Rome fell to the very barbarians they had hired into their army as mercenaries, the new *Chappie* sci-fi movie features robots that act as police.

Today, we are captive to technologies we've developed, which no longer serve us as much as rule us. Perhaps not yet as dire as the *Chappie*, but just as pervasively disarming:

- E-mail and texting have replaced human conversation to an alarming degree . . . while enabling our children to sext pictures of their privates.
- Automated voice response systems shield companies from their customers, making it maddeningly difficult to get a human on the phone to answer a question or address a problem.

- My "smart" TV shuts itself off to conserve electricity—even in the middle of a movie.

Ever since the Luddite uprising against the British industrial revolution two centuries ago, people have opposed the arrival of technologies that threatened to change the way they work and live.

I'm not alone in questioning if today's technologies are paying the promised dividends—such as more free time. German philosopher Martin Heidegger wrote as long ago as 1954 that, "Everywhere we remain unfree and chained to technology."

A few years ago Yale University professor David Gelernter called for anti-Internet activism:

> *... not in the sense of a destructive Luddite movement that makes it a practice of destroying computers, but a group of intellectual dissent that asks us to slow down, that asks us to evaluate what we have achieved, that asks us in practical terms what we have gotten for our money, asks us what environment our children are growing up in.*

Another way to put it, as movie scientist Deon says to Chappie the robot, "I created you, but I might not survive you."

# 50

## *All It Takes*

It's the time of Passover and Easter, when large numbers of people around the world are mindful of the biblical admonition to "Be holy, for I, the Lord, am holy."

Be holy? Easier said than done. Or is it?

Some scholars estimate that it was more than 3,300 years ago when God gave Moses the Torah, with a full program to fulfill His call to holiness—more than 600 admonitions.

According to one story, the revered Rabbi Hillel, two thousand years ago, was asked to explain his religion—within the time one could stand on a single leg. Hillel's riposte: "That which is hateful to you, do not do to your neighbor. That is the whole Torah; the rest is the explanation."

Almost three thousand years ago, the earliest texts of The Book of the Dead came down to us from Egypt's Old Kingdom. The Hall of Maat was described in these writings, where divine judgment of the dead was performed with the aid of a simple balance. On the pan of one scale was the dead one's heart, representing his conscience. On the other pan lay a feather, representing truth, justice, and morality. To gain access to the eternal Fields of Peace, the heart could not weigh more than the feather.

According to the Egyptian text, one man under judgment pleaded his case this way: "I have never made anyone cry. I have never caused anyone to be afraid."

Jesus Christ taught this: "You shall love the Lord, your God, with all your heart, with all your soul, and with all your mind. This is the greatest and the first commandment. The second is like it: You shall love your neighbor as yourself. The whole law and the prophets depend on these two commandments."

French philosopher Simone Weil, who died during the darkest days of World War II, left us this: "People who treat as equal those whose relative strength is far below their own truly give them a gift of the quality of human beings."

Then there's Mother Teresa, who is today regarded as holy by believers and nonbelievers alike. Someone once told me a story about a prominent man who sought her spiritual advice. Mother Teresa is said to have told him: "Spend half an hour each day with your Maker, then do what you know is right."

Are you finding a common denominator in three millennia of pondering what it is that gives human life transcendent value? Are you getting a glimpse of the wonderful world it would be if humankind lived according to these words?

To my way of thinking, if we can close out our lives saying nothing more than, "I never made anyone cry, I never made anyone feel afraid," we were of value. We were holy.

That's all it takes. Except that it takes our all.

# 51

## *Number One and Number Two*

They are Number One and Number Two at what they do. What they do is earn billions and billions of dollars. And that's just an estimate.

It's the Millennials. Again. These people—born between 1977 and 1992—are going online to shop for insurance coverage. This is forcing insurers who once sold through agents to advertise directly to consumers. Insurance is a mature industry. This means that in order to grow, insurance companies must steal market share from one another.

Believe it or not, insurance companies are often perceived as cold and uncaring. So they are turning to what's known as "brand personality campaigns," to change the negative perception by identifying with characters who convey warmth, humor, and credibility.

The Number One and Number Two brand personalities of 2015 are the "Geico Gecko" and "Progressive Flo."

A reptile? Can a lizard be warm and cuddly? Yes, according to a 2011 study for *Advertising Age*. More than 90 percent of consumers recognize the Gecko—and the company.

How does one come up with a reptile as a spokesperson? Geico's name was often mispronounced "gecko," and as the ad agency was brainstorming, someone doodled a gecko. Voila! The Gecko came to life and made his debut during the 1999–2000 television season.

About the same time, that dopey duck appeared—the one who tries to convince us that ducks don't say "quack" but "aflac." The ad agency came up with the duck because they had been having a hard time remembering the company's name—American Family Life Assurance Company. One day, one of them asked, "What's the name of the account we're pitching?" A colleague replied, "It's Aflac! Aflac, Aflac, Aflac!" Someone said he sounded like a duck, and the idea was hatched. The company's name recognition soared from 11 percent to 94 percent, and sales of plush Aflac Ducks today raise millions for the treatment and research of childhood cancer.

These faux characters have become part of our social fabric. Don't you love khaki-clad Jake from State Farm? He and the other brand personalities even have Twitter followers and Facebook pages. The Aflac Duck has a spot in Macy's Thanksgiving Parade. At Halloween, you can buy a Flo costume.

In November 2014, Progressive aired its hundredth Flo commercial. Flo has evolved from humble beginnings as a cashier into a love interest, a reality star, and an insurance pusher. She's "different than anything else in an industry that is literally an arms race right now," says the firm's chief marketing executive (who joined Progressive from Aflac, by the way), who talks about the fictional character as if it were real.

Let's overlook the fact that a major corporation's chief marketing officer doesn't know the difference between *literally* and *figuratively*. He must have been absent the day they taught that in fifth grade. But an arms race?

"We wanted to kick Flo's ass," said an Allstate ad agency exec—obviously another class act—when they launched their "Mayhem" campaign in response to being ranked fourth in advertising spending behind Geico, State Farm, and Progressive.

The Mayhem guy is a metaphor for any disaster that might befall you, and he warns you to buy insurance. Mr. Mayhem boosted Allstate to third place as most-recognized insurance advertising character, behind The Gecko and The Girl.

All this sounds silly to us grown-ups. But mega-money is up for grabs. In 2013, the US life and health insurance industry alone generated revenue of $783.9 billion. Billion.

# 52

## *Uniforms Are Supposed to Be Uniform*

With opening day of the baseball season this month came the sloppy spectacle of players wearing different versions of their team uniform. Pants knee-high . . . pants ankle-high . . . cuffs dragging on the turf.

Perhaps no other sport has produced as nostalgic a uniform as baseball:

- The first official baseball uniform, adopted in 1849 by the Knickerbocker Base Ball Club of New York City, consisted of a white flannel shirt, blue wool pants, and a straw hat.
- In 1868 the Cincinnati Red Stockings introduced knickers, which were little changed since the early 1800s. The stockings often became a team signature. The Cincinnati Red Stockings in the 1860s paved the way, followed by the St. Louis Brown Stockings and the Chicago White Stockings.
- Since 1976 alone, however, some four thousand different styles have been worn by major league baseball players.

And now we must suffer both knee-length and full-length pants on the field at the same time.

You know what this really means? Still another English word has lost its meaning.

*Awesome*, for instance, has lost its original meaning of *fearsome*. A *guru* is an *expert* instead of its accurate translation as *teacher*. And now *uniform* has a new and totally opposite meaning.

Since 1746, *Webster*, has described a *uniform* as "dress of a distinctive design or fashion worn by members of a particular group and serving as a means of identification; broadly: distinctive or characteristic clothing."

Sue Wicks, the Women's Basketball Hall of Famer, once said, "Everyone is an outsider until you're given a uniform."

Not anymore. Today *uniform* connotes dress that is habitually worn as an expression of individuality. Instead of defining your membership in something larger and grander than yourself, a uniform now attempts to define the grandeur of your individuality:

- The signature look of author Tom Wolfe (*Bonfire of the Vanities*) is an ice-cream-white suit.
- Apple founder Steve Jobs wore a black mock turtleneck—always.
- Facebook Chairman and CEO Mark Zuckerberg follows suit with his jeans and hoodies.

IBM's "unwritten" dress code of vested blue suit, white shirt, sincere tie, and wing-tipped shoes grew out of founder Thomas J. Watson's reaction to the typical salesman's snappy getup of the 1920s—a look not unlike Robert Preston's in the 1957 Broadway production of *The Music Man*.

Although IBM sold elementary accounting machines in those early days, Mr. Watson differentiated the IBM sales force from the gaggle with a look that projected an organization of global scope and gravity—the "International Business Machines Corporation."

During my own years at IBM, my humble group of speechwriters occupied prime space near the CEO's suite. Whenever we were summoned to a meeting with him, we would don our jackets before heading to his office.

We might not have been sales people representing IBM in front of its customers, but our "uniform" made us feel a prideful part of an organization that back then truly was one of global scope and gravity.

Uniforms used to mean more—before the era of free agents and universal individuality. For example:

- In a time before athletes "trash-talked" their opponents in advance of a contest, Hall of Famer Ryne Sandberg—whose .989 fielding percentage remains the major league record at second base—said, "You never, ever disrespect your opponent or your teammates or your organization or your manager and never, ever your uniform."
- Joe Torre, who guided the Yankees to four World Series titles, said that as a kid growing up in Brooklyn, "I knew what the Dodgers uniform represented."
- And Dodgers manager Tommy Lasorda used to say, "I love doubleheaders. That way I get to keep my uniform on longer."

Jarod Kintz, author of *This Book Is Not FOR SALE*, summed it up nicely:

*"We all wear uniforms, even if we're conforming to unconformity. People who try so hard to look different end up looking the same as all the other people who try so hard to look different."*

# 53

## *Cooking for One*

Sophia Loren reportedly said, *"Everything you see, I owe to spaghetti."* With credentials like hers, I figure, how wrong could she be?

So I signed up for a short course in Italian cooking at the celebrated Truro Center for the Arts at Castle Hill on Cape Cod.

In chatting with the other students, I discovered that there is general agreement that "cooking for one" is not one of life's pleasures.

I found myself odd man out for two reasons. First, in two of the three classes, I was the sole male student. Second, I like cooking, whether for others or for just one. Few things focus my mind as much as cooking—and crowd out the cares of the day.

The preparation of food demands total concentration—mental and tactile—in making accurate measurements, gauging the feel of dough as you knead it, monitoring the temperature of skillets and saucepans and ovens.

More than a half-century after Julia Child introduced French cuisine to the American household, television networks have discovered that food shows can be popular and profitable. But food channels often feature snarling celebrity chefs far removed from the elegant and gracious Julia. Television also has turned the art of cooking into ridiculous competitions, just as almost every other art form I can think of has been made competitive, from dance to poetry.

But cooking for yourself, in the quiet of your kitchen, follows the Zen precept of looking after yourself and the space you occupy. At the Zen Garland spiritual center in Airmont, New York, for example, students are taught to practice mindfulness in all their activities. Says the center's spiritual director, Roshi Paul Genki Kahn:

*Zen is the realization that the sacred is in each and every moment of life—in the most ordinary actions like eating, sleeping, even sweeping the floors.*

But Zen thought seems to place more attention on the eating than the preparation. Devoted Zen practitioners eat food that's as close as possible to its natural state—requiring little if any cooking or other preparation. Buddhist monks go out in the streets each morning carrying empty dishes that adherents fill with food offerings.

My Castle Hill classes were taught by Chef Michael Ceraldi, who's worked with influential chefs in Italian cuisine in New York and in Italy. He came to Cape Cod in 2010 as executive chef of *Dalla Cucina* ("Best Italian" 2011 in *Yankee* magazine). In 2013 he opened a Provincetown pop-up that finished the season as Trip Advisor's top-rated Cape restaurant. He has since opened his seasonal restaurant, *Ceraldi's,* at Wellfleet harbor in 2015, with a multi-course tasting menu that changes each evening.

My classes with Chef Michael began with making fresh pasta, ravioli and tomato sauce. Then came potato gnocchi and a spinach-ricotta version known as *malfatti*. We ended the course making risotto and the risotto-and-mozzarella-filled croquettes called *arancini*.

All this was a far cry from my days of producing corporate events during which we always had to serve "safe" fare—meaning menu items that appealed to a diverse group of men and women sometimes numbering close to a thousand.

I'm in Vieques for this month, tending to things at my house here. So with my wife far north on Cape Cod, I'm enjoying cooking for one. What's best—nobody else is here to count how many *arancini* I stuff into my mouth.

# 54

## *Why, Women?*

Perhaps you have to be a father of girls to understand the clutch in my throat when my daughters tell me about the bullying they've suffered because some guy judged them not a winner—therefore worthless.

So on this Mother's Day weekend, I'm remembering 1968, when hundreds of women went to Atlantic City to picket the Miss America Pageant . . . and put Women's Liberation into the public consciousness. And I'm wondering why, women, a half-century afterward, are so many of you still allowing so many males to define you?

Like this, for example.

*The Shriver Report Snapshot: An Insight into the 21st Century Man,* published in May 2015, questioned 818 mostly American, heterosexual males older than eighteen. They were asked which traits "they wanted" most in a wife or partner—and in a daughter:

- Intelligence ranked at the top for both.

- Independence and strength were far more valued in a daughter than a wife.
- Being principled was seen as more important for a daughter than a partner.
- Attractiveness, sweetness, and nurturing were far more valued in a partner than a daughter.
- Two-thirds wanted an independent daughter; only a third wanted an independent partner.

When I consider this, I can't help picturing women as candy vending machines from which men make their selections: attractiveness today, independence tomorrow . . . Snickers today, Hershey bars tomorrow.

The same year as the Miss America protest, to trivialize what the Liberation movement was all about, the cigarette guys introduced Virginia Slims with the tag, "You've Come a Long Way, Baby."

In 1969 came Philip Roth's breakthrough *Portnoy's Complaint*. The novel enshrined a slab of raw liver in the hand of its randy young protagonist.

In many circles in the 1970s, recalls women's historian Jone Johnson Lewis, "*. . . being sexually free meant primarily being more sexually available to men, and still doing all the laundry, cooking, and housecleaning. . . . One Illinois legislator was quoted . . . calling feminists 'braless, brainless broads.'*"

When men disrespect women like this—or abuse them physically or emotionally or in hiring or in compensation—we all are assaulted.

Oxford University student Ione Wells recently wrote in an open letter to an attempted rapist:

> *You did not just attack me that night. I am a daughter, I am a friend, I am a girlfriend, I am a pupil, I am a cousin, I am a niece, I am a neighbour, I am the employee who served everyone down the road coffee in the café under the railway. All the people who form those relations to me make up my community, and you assaulted every single one of them.*

Even someone as successful as Oscar-winner Helen Hunt feels the overwhelming challenge of being a woman today.

In a *Huffington Post* interview, she noted that fewer roles go to older actresses today—not because of age, but because they are women: "I'm tired of the billboard where she's barely in her underwear and they're selling a watch or something. . . . I'm over it, to be honest."

I'm over it, too, Helen.

I'm over seeing twenty-year-old LPGA golfer Lexi Thompson topless on the cover of the May 2015 *Golf Digest* . . . with the jacket around her neck dangling down just enough to cover her nipples.

I'm over the annual *Sports Illustrated* "swimsuit issue" . . . all bulbous breasts and bikini bottoms and pubic bones.

I'm over the Victoria's Secret company—whose stock-in-trade is young women's bodies—shamefully refusing to make bras for women once they've had mastectomies.

For Thoreau, a notable bachelor, the morning hour at Walden Pond was a time for poetry and art. But he added: "To affect the quality of the day, that is the highest of arts."

Could he have been urging all of us—women especially—to fashion our life into a work of art day by day, by means of our own perception of ourselves?

# 55

## *The Next-Larger Context*

There are three brothers.

The youngest delivers milk to institutional customers each night until he slips on ice in the darkness, suffers a hairline fracture of a collarbone, and dies days later from a resultant blood clot.

The middle sibling leaves college three-fourths of the way to his baccalaureate and finds work as a bill collector until he succumbs, an amputee, to adult-onset diabetes.

The third brother, the oldest, is me.

In this country, we raise our children to accept the romantic notion that "if you can dream it, you can do it."

That's bumper sticker thinking.

I remember meeting Matt Biondi, who explained how he became one of the all-time greatest Olympic gold medal swimmers:

*There are literally hundreds of thousands of swimmers who have the ability to win a gold medal, and hundreds of thousands more who have the motivation and drive. But there are only three or four who have taken the time to sit down with themselves and decide what they have to do to win.*

Notice that the dream starts with a gift, usually an accident of birth. You're musically talented. Or intellectually acute. Or tall. Or good-looking.

The point is, there's more to achievement than determination and drive. There has to be luck. But most of all, there has to be willingness to change—to run the risk of pursuing the next larger thing.

Eliel Saarinen was a Finnish architect famous in the early twentieth century for his art nouveau buildings. His guiding principle:

*Always design a thing by considering it in its next larger context—a chair in a room, a room in a house, a house in an environment, an environment in a city plan.*

My brothers and I came from the same house, same ethnic and religious background, same parental upbringing. But I was the brother who got the lucky breaks—and acted on them.

I was such a dutiful altar server, for example, that I was offered entry to a minor seminary, with classes taken at a New England prep school. It meant leaving home just shy of fourteen. But I ran with it, and entered a larger, vastly different world from the factories and refineries of my New Jersey hometown.

Later, as a newspaper reporter with a growing family, I realized that my salary wasn't easily paying the bills. I answered a blind ad for a corporate job. It turned out to be IBM. It meant relocation, and starting over again as a small fish in a very big, multinational pond.

Twenty years later, when IBM needed to downsize, the company offered a huge incentive for employees to leave. Divorcing myself from this stunningly powerful and paternalistic corporation was a move I had never entertained. But my decision to resign led to the establishment of my own consultancy, Executive Media, now celebrating its twentieth year.

In each case, opportunity presented itself.

In each case, I accepted change, disruption, and risk.

In each case, I stepped into the next-larger context.

# 56

## The Coywolves of Cape Cod

Threaded through the *Jurassic Park* movies is the romantic thesis that "life finds a way." It's happening on Cape Cod right under our noses. Our little spit of sandbar has become home to a new kind of animal.

They are called coywolves. Highly intelligent and adaptable, they are very sociable, mate for life, and live in family packs.

These hybrids are bigger and more wolf-like than the coyotes of the west—some 62 percent coyote, 27 percent wolf, and 11 percent dog. Eighty pounds heavy and double the size of a typical coyote.

"Evolution in action," Trent University geneticist Bradley White calls it. "In many ways, this animal is a creation of human impact on the planet."

As human settlers populated the Northeast during the past few hundred years, decimating the forests and ridding the land of wolves, western coyotes migrated through Canada to take over the territory that had been inhabited by wolves. In Canada's Algonquin Park, protected wolves bred with the migrating coyotes and by 1919 had spawned the hybrids that now live among us.

Massachusetts is the third most densely populated state in the country, losing an estimated forty acres of land a day to development. In wooded areas, coywolves eat deer, mice, rabbits, and other small animals and rodents. The deer and mice they consume are key because the incidence of Lyme disease explodes when deer and mice populations increase.

As wooded habitat decreases, however, coywolves are drawn to urban and suburban neighborhoods, where they associate food with people and lose their natural fear of humans.

A 2013 study found that even Ohio coyotes had wolf genes, a surprising finding that suggests coywolves are moving south from New England through the mid-Atlantic area and circling back westward. At least one coywolf has been captured in Manhattan's Central Park, and two thousand are estimated to live in greater Chicago. Rick Perry, the former Texas governor, shot a coyote while jogging.

*The Journal News* of Westchester County, just north of New York City, ran a huge Page One story in June 2015 headlined ON THE PROWL IN SUBURBIA. The report struck a typically knee-jerk tone about the danger coyotes pose to pets and small children. Residents of this tony suburban area are now setting leg traps on their manicured lawns.

But biologist Jonathan Way has a very different take:

*These animals—even the ones living in urban areas—provide such a minor risk compared to other risks in our everyday activities that they do not even qualify as a danger. Yet they are slaughtered in staggering numbers.*

Way has devoted his career to studying coyotes around Boston and Cape Cod. It was he who proposed the "coywolf" name, and he is today a voice for their protection.

A quick review of Massachusetts hunting regulations finds that governmental bodies don't even acknowledge coywolves. Only coyotes are named, and these can be legally hunted down—year-round and in unlimited numbers—using anything from dogs and imitation calls to handguns and archery. Massachusetts even allows people to place bait on their lawns at night and fire from their house at a feeding creature.

Says Way:

*This has to be the most unethical, non-sporting practice imaginable. How can this even remotely be called hunting? Sadly, I am now learning that many people kill coyotes like this and I would subjectively guess that over half of the 'coyotes' in Massachusetts are killed this way every year.*

# 57

## A Father's Day Gift to Women

On this Father's Day weekend, when lots of men are the recipients of ties, favorite meals, or golf outings, I'm wondering about the opposite. What is it that women want most from a man, whether he's father, husband or friend? It's a gift they never actually put into words and ask for, but it's one they deeply desire.

I found the answer to my question in a song from the 1965 Broadway musical, *Man of La Mancha*.

It's the tale of Don Quixote, a Spanish knight-errant thought to be mad because of his naïve idealism, who falls in love with a wanton serving wench named Aldonza. He recognizes her inner beauty and believes her to be the lady Dulcinea, to whom he swears eternal love and loyalty. Aldonza scoffs and tells him to see her as she really is—and to stop calling her "Dulcinea."

But Quixote persists. He does, in fact, see her as she really is. But it's not in the disdainful way that she sees herself.

"I see heaven when I see thee, Dulcinea," he sings, and continues:

*Dulcinea . . . Dulcinea . . .*
*I have sought thee, sung thee,*
*Dreamed thee, Dulcinea!*
*Now I've found thee,*
*And the world shall know thy glory,*
*Dulcinea . . . Dulcinea!*

As the story unfolds, Aldonza comes to accept the real woman that Quixote sees in her, and she can no longer bear to think of herself as anyone but—Dulcinea.

Psychologist Mollie Marti updates the idea: "Let others see their own greatness when looking in your eyes."

To have this kind of effect on others, however, requires first that you are comfortable and confident in yourself. "The privilege of a lifetime is to become who you truly are," as Jung put it.

In other words, to be authentic. To be real. To be able to say, along with Quixote, "I am I."

But it's not always easy.

"Real isn't how you are made," Margery Williams has the Skin Horse say in her classic children's story, *The Velveteen Rabbit*.

> *"It's a thing that happens to you. When a child loves you for a long, long time, not just to play with, but REALLY loves you, then you become Real."*
>
> *"Does it hurt?" asked the Rabbit.*
>
> *"Sometimes," said the Skin Horse, for he was always truthful. "When you are Real you don't mind being hurt."*

New Zealand writer Sue Fitzmaurice says a man is authentic when he's:

- Free from hypocrisy
- Unafraid to reveal his vulnerabilities
- Confident to walk away from situations where he can't be himself

- Awake to his own feelings
- Free from the opinions of others
- Accepting and loving of himself

These are the qualities of a man of gentleness, the makings of emotional maturity—what women tell me they want most in a man.

For example, songwriter and poet Charlotte Eriksson: "Some people make you want to be a better person, and that, for me, is the purest form of love."

And that, for me, is my idea of a Father's Day gift for women.

# 58

## *To Correct the Past*

They promised a world of total pleasure. There was only one thing you couldn't have—your thirtieth birthday.

Sound like science fiction?

It was. The 1976 movie, *Logan's Run*, was set in an idyllic future that suffered only one drawback: your life must end when you turned thirty.

I'm old enough to remember 1964 and the Free Speech Movement at UC Berkeley, when student Jack Weinberg explained that, " . . . we don't trust anyone over thirty."

Now, on the far side of thirty myself, I'm wary of anyone *under* thirty. The under-thirty crowd acts as if the present exists to correct the past.

A study reported by Walter Frick in April 2013 found that those under the age of 35 represented a significant proportion of founders in *The Wall Street Journal's* billion-dollar club, with the average age coming in at 31.

To my way of thinking, this means if you haven't reached a leadership position in your field by forty—especially in business—you may as well swallow the pill.

It seems that forty is the new sixty-five.

Perhaps this is why, even more than every generation before them, today's youth consider themselves enlightened. Gone and forgotten is any presumption that their elders might possess a thing called wisdom.

Consequently, marketers pretty much write off the sixty-five+ demographic. They see this senescent group forming no major purchasing bloc, wielding no significant voting clout, and simply too set in their ways to be of much use at all.

And there are so many of these curmudgeonly codgers doddering about!

A Census Bureau Report released in March 2015 forecasts that within the next fifteen years, all the baby boomers will have reached age sixty-five, making one in five Americans senior citizens—up from one in seven last year.

There's no question, of course, that major work can be achieved by the very young. In his book, *What the Dog Saw,* Malcolm Gladwell notes that:

- Orson Welles filmed *Citizen Kane* at twenty-five
- Herman Melville published *Moby-Dick* at thirty-two
- Mozart wrote his breakthrough Piano Concerto in E-flat Major, no. 9, at twenty-one

But let's look at some equally compelling facts:

- Forty-two percent of Robert Frost's anthologized poems were written after he was fifty
- Alfred Hitchcock made *Dial M for Murder, Rear Window, To Catch a Thief, Vertigo, North by Northwest,* and *Psycho* after he was fifty-four
- Mark Twain published *Adventures of Huckleberry Finn* at forty-nine, and Daniel Defoe wrote *Robinson Crusoe* at fifty-eight

And there's the testimony of no one less than Georges Clemenceau. Clemenceau, you'll remember, was the French statesman and journalist who, as premier, was a major contributor to the World War I Allied victory and a framer of the postwar Treaty of Versailles. He said: "All that I know I learned after I was thirty."

My latest run-in with the whippersnappers (*"noun:* an unimportant but offensively presumptuous person, especially a young one") started with a promotional e-mail my company received last week from an event venue search-and-booking company.

"Woohoo!" the message began. "We've launched our new look for desktop!"

I wrote back: "Dear Kids: I don't read mail with 'Woohoo' in the subject line. Grow up."

# 59

*For Better, For Worse*

*We've moved from a culture in which we were told that sex is bad and dangerous and should only be had under very particular circumstances, to one in which we're told that sex is pretty great, really—and if you're not doing it, something must be wrong with you. . . . The ideal of waiting until marriage is really only common among very religious people and it's something they struggle with.*

That's Rachel Hills talking about the result of six years spent interviewing young people about their sex lives—and the disconnect between the fantasy they were promised and their actual experience. Her book, *The Sex Myth*, was published the same July 2015 week that I saw a wedding take place at our beach on Cape Cod Bay.

The juncture of these two events has me thinking about cohabitation, weddings, and marriage.

*Wedding* comes down to us from the Old English *weddian* . . . which is rooted in the Scots word *wed*, a "pledge" . . . from the Latin *vas*, "surety," which connotes a formal assurance that an agreement will be fulfilled.

So "wedding" means something ongoing.

Not just one day, but a way of life.

Not just a party that has to be perfect, but a surety whose fulfillment flowers in every present moment.

Fully ten years ago, more than two-thirds of married couples in the United States admitted living together before marrying.

Why not?

Cohabitation is a test bed for harmonious interrelations, lifestyle affinity, sexual rapport.

But—I don't get it.

Isn't this a case of compatibility eclipsing commitment?

Come the wedding day, there's no "there" there. They are already wed in all but name and law.

Commentators have gone so far as to equate premarital cohabitation to test-driving a car before buying it.

The happy, expectant faces of the newlyweds' family and friends that I saw at the beach this week manifested hope. Hope that this marriage will be for better, for richer, for healthier. Hope that this couple's commitment will complement their compatibility.

I'm of the generation in which virginity was valued, sex before marriage was frowned on, and a lifelong relationship was assumed. My wife and I, for example, met when we were studying at Fordham University and married within months of graduation. In a few months, we will mark a half-century of marriage.

Traditional marriage has been called a Hail Mary pass to a life with someone you hope you can live with happily.

But my wife and I have found, instead, that our marriage is an unending process of discovery. Like any kind of relationship, marriage progresses through three phases:

- Romance, when all is fresh and exciting as we discover the ever-unfolding wonderfulness of the other—and cannot abide being apart

- Disillusionment, when we discover the chinks and the cracks—and wonder what we ever saw in the other
- Joy, when we discover the depth of the other—and become soul mates

With a new anticancer medicine leaving my wife exhausted just by crossing a room, I'm discovering that I feel not a burden but a joy in caring for her. In turn, she is discovering new things about me—the least of which that I can serve up a decent dinner.

For us right now, it truly is as we pledged on our wedding day, "for better, for worse, for richer, for poorer, in sickness and in health, until death do us part."

# 60

## A Millennial Pop Quiz

*I really do not know that anything has ever been
more exciting than diagramming sentences.*

**—GERTRUDE STEIN**

S tein might have been writing with her tongue in her cheek, of course,
but diagramming sentences was and still is taken very seriously by a lot
of people.

*Investor's Business Daily*, for example, reported the experience of
Joseph R. Mallon, Jr., when he was chairman and CEO of Measurement
Specialties, Inc.

Whenever he was faced with a complex problem, he harkened back to
the Sisters of the Immaculate Conception, who taught him the art of diagramming a sentence when he was in high school. It's an analytical process
he applied to tackling tough business issues.

*Take (the issue) apart into its component parts. Make sure all the components fit together well. They've got to be well chosen, fit together, and make sense. There are few problems that can't be solved that way.*

Things that once were very important to us fall into insignificance and obsolescence with the passage of generations.

I was reminded of this when my grandson, a smart-as-a-whip university student who's not shy with the ladies, stumbled over this sentence from my latest book, *Fat Guy in a Fat Boat*:

> *. . . like the lacy hem of a pretty girl's slip.*

He actually had to ask his mother, "Mom, what's a girl's slip?"

The next time I see him, I'll ask him if he knows Paul McCartney was in a band before Wings.

He probably doesn't even know there was a band named Wings.

Then there's my California *amiga*, Fawn, who told me she has a thirty-year-old woman friend who's never heard of Gloria Steinem.

All this sounded like it would make a good game for Millennials—and anyone else who doesn't know what to do with an S&H Green Stamp.

So here is my "Pop Quiz for Millennials." It features multiple-choice and fill-in-the-blanks questions:

1. *Windsor* can mean:
   a. A model of Rolls Royce automobile
   b. A style of necktie knot
   c. The name of a hybrid rose
   d. None of the above
   e. All of the above

2. *Spaldeen* is:
   a. A brand of soccer ball
   b. An alloy of aluminum and bauxite
   c. A town in Wyoming
   d. None of the above
   e. All of the above

3.  A *slide rule* can be used for:
    a.  Multiplication
    b.  Division
    c.  Logarithms
    d.  None of the above
    e.  All of the above

4.  A *siren* is:
    a.  A figure in Greek mythology
    b.  A dangerously enticing woman
    c.  A device used in surgical procedures
    d.  None of the above
    e.  All of the above

5.  A *peep show* might be:
    a.  Erotic images viewed from a coin-operated booth
    b.  A diorama composed of marshmallow Peeps
    c.  A Viennese children's toy
    d.  None of the above
    e.  All of the above

6.  Old-timers used to say, "A rolling stone gathers no _____."
7.  In the fifties, a good secretary was able to take dictation in _____.
8.  ___ _____ was a manufacturing process developed in the eighties to show that products were defect-free.
9.  A _____-__-_____ salesman might sell anything from brushes to vacuums to encyclopedias.
10. Under a dress, a girl wore a slip; under a skirt, she wore a _____.

**Answers:** 1. A style of necktie knot; 2. None of the above; 3. All of the above; 4. A dangerously enticing woman; 5. All of the above; 6. moss; 7. shorthand; 8. Six Sigma; 9. door-to-door; 10. crinoline.

# 61

## *The Assault on Architecture*

There's something about architecture that arrests us, often without our being aware. Even as Jesus was about to bring Lazarus back to life, he asked for help in removing the stone that sealed the tomb.

This was something he could have accomplished with a flick of a finger. Perhaps this divine example was what has always prompted churches and monasteries to be constructed of stone—the hard element of the earth—even as they sought to touch heaven.

Forests were the first temples, as James C. Snyder writes in his *Introduction to Architecture*, where "men grasped their first idea of architecture." In Ukraine, the nation of my heritage, churches built of wood are traditional and still being built throughout the worldwide Ukrainian diaspora.

But most builders of religious edifices turn to stone and brick—components more lasting than wood—in order to leave a more lasting legacy of their worship, their art and their view of a transcendent world.

I'm hesitant, though, about the architectural legacy we're leaving for future generations.

I'm anxious mostly because the bulk of today's architecture reflects in large part a society of commercialism, stepping to the beat of corporate marketers.

Almost two centuries ago, Victor Hugo said it better than I:

*". . . the greatest productions of architecture are not so much the work of individuals as of society—the offspring rather of national efforts than the outcome of a particular genius . . . ."*

The study of architecture is a lifelong endeavor. I am not equipped to present a scholarly comment on the current state of affairs of the buildings we are constructing.

So I'll leave it to Ada Louise Huxtable, winner of the first Pulitzer Prize for architecture criticism. In her landmark book, *On Architecture: Collected Reflections on a Century of Change*, she writes:

*Today, when so much seems to conspire to reduce life and feeling to the most deprived and demeaning bottom line, it is more important than ever that we receive that extra dimension of dignity or delight and the elevated sense of self that the art of building can provide through the nature of the places where we live and work. What counts more than style is whether architecture improves our experience of the built world; whether it makes us wonder why we never noticed places in quite this way before.*

# 62

## *Yada Yada Yada*

All I had to say was "yada yada yada" and I became old pals with the stranger next to me in line at the Truro Post Office.

He had wanted to make a point about something we were chatting about, and he asked me if I ever watched *Seinfeld*.

I blurted, "Yada yada yada."

That's all it took.

The line was a lengthy one—locals, summer residents, assorted tourists to Cape Cod. So by the time I reached the postal clerk at the counter, I had learned that my new friend lived in neighboring Provincetown and days earlier had been struck on crowded Commercial Street by a bicycle driven by John Waters, the celeb film director who has a home there.

What happened to me in the post office was a powerful demonstration of frame of reference. What writers call *allusion*—like a shorthand to explain an idea.

Each of us has a unique frame of reference that stems from our individual IQ, age, race, gender, culture, education, experiences, social conditioning, and more.

These factors form a filter through which we view the world and create our personal perception of reality.

But if each of us has an exclusive perception of reality, how do we communicate, do business with one another, and have meaningful relationships with others?

This is where allusions come in. For communication to be successful, we rely on similarities that are based on shared experiences, interests and agreements. They provide the connections.

Allusions to idioms, names and plotlines from the Seinfeld TV series that ran from 1989 to 1998 have become common in many conversations I've had. Seinfeld scenarios repeatedly come up as shared reference points that make for immediate and impactful illustration:

*No soup for you!*
*Not that there's anything wrong with that!*
*There was shrinkage!*

Where Greek mythology gave us allusions to an Adonis, a harpy and a muse, Shakespeare coined an Iago, a Romeo and a Shylock. Seinfeld's offerings? Soup Nazi, sponge-worthy and master of his domain.

If you think I'm over-analyzing what was never intended to be more than a comedy, consider this.

Medical students at Rutgers Robert Wood Johnson Medical School are learning about psychiatric disorders by studying Seinfeld.

"It's a show about a pretty significant amount of psychiatry," says Dr. Anthony Tobia.

He's created a database of teaching points from the show's episodes, something that took him two years. Third- and fourth-year medical students are assigned to watch two episodes a week and then gather to discuss the psychopathology demonstrated on each.

"You have a very diverse group of personality traits that are maladaptive on the individual level," Tobia said. "When you get these friends together, the dynamic creates a plot: Jerry's obsessive-compulsive traits combined with Kramer's schizoid traits, with Elaine's inability to forge meaningful relationships, and George being egocentric."

I have to agree with one of his students, who said: "I had watched the show as a kid, certainly not understanding it to an extent that I think I do now."

# 63

## *Gaudeamus, Igitur?*

Bill Gates, Michael Dell, Mark Zuckerberg, Coco Chanel, Steve Jobs, Oprah. All of them household names. All of them lack a college degree. Yet . . . a recent employment ad for a Zamboni driver for the New York Islanders hockey team requires a college degree.

A young woman of my acquaintance was a contract worker for several months in the marketing department of a nationally known company. During her tenure, she caught an error that may prove to save the company tens to hundreds of thousands of dollars. Her boss loved her and began the process of hiring her as a full-time employee.

That's when Human Resources put the kibosh on the offer. The reason? My friend had left college—more than twenty years ago—before obtaining a degree. Two decades of corporate experience and superb performance as a contract employee didn't matter to HR.

Lori Davila, top US resume writer, interviewing coach, and McGraw-Hill author, told me this:

*High-performing, competitive organizations hire people who can solve critical business challenges when there is no obvious answer. This requires focusing on a candidate's valuable and relevant experience. A college degree by itself does not reveal a candidate's full potential and certainly does not guarantee performance. It's critical to hire the right person, not the right degree.*

Kwame Anthony Appiah, who teaches philosophy at New York University, nicely summed up what I'm saying: "What you can do and who you can be—the qualities of your skills and of your soul—are two separate questions that aren't quite separable."

Richard J. Light, a professor at Harvard Graduate School of Education, reported last month on its novel, noncredit seminar called "Reflecting on Your Life."

The seminar gets first-year students thinking about questions beyond career:

- *What does it mean to live a good life?*
- *What about a productive life?*
- *How about a happy life?*
- *How might I think about these ideas if the answers conflict with one another?*
- *How do I use my time here at college to build on the answers to these tough questions?*

The Harvard seminar is an encouraging step toward returning college to the transformational experience it's meant to be instead of the vocational training camp it's become.

# 64

## *Three Women*

"I've been hit, spit on, and cursed at. But I love it."

Something out of *Fifty Shades of Grey*?

No. It was a hospital nurse here on Cape Cod talking about her job.

During my wife's recent hospital stay, she had a round-the-clock rotation of nurses attending to her. They all seemed to share a common trait—a work ethic that can be best described as uncommon.

One, for example, specializes in phlebotomy. She drives fifty-three miles each way between home and job, raises three kids—the youngest four months old—and is enrolled in an eight-year program to become a midwife.

A second nurse is mother to three daughters—whom she home-schooled—holds a black belt in karate, teaches martial arts, and operates a catering business.

The third nurse is the one I quoted above in describing some of the experiences she's had with patients in the throes of addiction. "I've been hit, spit on, and cursed at. But I love it. Even still, I wanted to help them."

Why do these nurses say "I love my job," with stress on the word *love*? Maybe because they find personal fulfillment—and joy—in serving others.

No matter how much we read, research, or discuss the reasons, the indicators consistently point to the same truth: it's the giver who receives the gift.

Here's Rabindranath Tagore, who was awarded the 1913 Nobel Prize in Literature:

*I slept and I dreamed that life is all joy. I woke and I saw that life is all service. I served and I saw that service is joy.*

This past week was rank with nauseating news about attacks on women:

- Two pro football players indicted for sexually assaulting a woman.
- A multi-millionaire basketball player and two of his friends sued by a woman for gang-raping her.
- The assassination of a female correspondent on live television.

The most disappointing news, to me, was yesterday's "not guilty" verdict in the case of a prep school senior accused of rape by a fifteen-year-old freshman.

According to *The New York Times* account, "The accuser, flanked by family members in the front row, broke into sobs," when the verdict was read.

The young man's attorney offered as defense: "He's not a saint." The logical conclusion is that it takes a saint to respect a woman's dignity.

So it was uplifting to meet those three Cape Cod nurses who are so driven to help others.

Picasso's 1921 *Three Women at the Spring* summons up the regard I feel for these nurses. The women in the painting seem larger-than-life, displaying strong, chiseled profiles, and statuesque contours.

With the spread of conformity and image-driven superficiality, the allure of an individuated woman in full possession of herself and her powers proves irresistible. Author Elizabeth Prioleau draws a compelling word image: "*We were born for plenitude and inner fulfillment.*"

# 65

## *We Are Song*

Why is it that the people most responsible for educating our children are so often on the wrong side of history? I'm talking about the federal, state, and local governments that have cast a collective thumbs-down on music education.

The No Child Left Behind Act of 2001 specifically included arts education as a core academic subject. But the legislation also elevated math, reading, and other subjects above other elements of the academic curriculum. Many school districts responded by de-emphasizing music and arts programs. The outcome? By 2010, according to the Department of Education, 40 percent of high schools no longer required coursework in these areas.

Music is a form of communication more magical than any other, from birds singing in treetops to whales sounding their eerie songs in ocean deeps.

Cave paintings depict people dancing, suggesting the presence of rhythmic music. The first musical instrument might have been a hollow stick to blow through and make sound.

Hebrew scripture is replete with references to vocal music, and King David's harp was one of the first stringed instruments, which he used as accompaniment when singing the many psalms that scholars believe he wrote. God rebuked a beleaguered Job: "Where were you when I laid the foundations of the earth . . . when the morning stars sang together?"

Ancient fathers of the Christian Church saw creation as the song of God. Gregory of Nyssa, for example, wrote in the fourth century, "Man is a musical composition, a wonderfully written hymn to powerful creative activity."

Stephen Freeman, an Orthodox priest and blogger, suggests that the utterance, "Let there be light," set the universe as a fugue. God sings. All of creation sings. Freeman calls music not entertainment, but "the very heart of creation. Man is not only a singer, but also a song. We are not only song, but also the song of God."

Contrary to state and local pressures to defund music and other arts, a nationwide study of 1,000 teachers and 800 parents earlier this year found strong support for music education at all grade levels.

"Striking a Chord: The Public's Hopes and Beliefs for K-12 Music Education in the United States 2015" identified strong majorities of teachers and parents who said music education should be funded, even at the expense of other programs and classes.

Eighty-three percent of teachers and 73 percent of parents said cutting music education is detrimental to students. They pointed to a dozen areas they would rather cut than music—school and district administration, standardized testing, athletics programs, and even Advanced Placement classes were all identified as better areas for budget cuts than music education.

How important is music to humankind? Peter Kreeft, professor of philosophy at Boston College, goes so far as to credit music as a proof of the existence of God:

*The first time I heard Beethoven's Ninth Symphony, I thought, 'I have ceased to be a human being. I am now the music itself. I will never get back into my body.'*

# 66

## The Zombie Muffin
## of Provincetown

I've discovered a new food group. Zombie Food.

Not food you feed *to* zombies, but food that *is* zombie—food that refuses to die within its appointed time.

I have on our kitchen counter a lemon-poppy seed muffin stump that is still soft and fresh after a month. I bought it for my wife at the Stop & Shop in Provincetown.

She ate the muffin top, and put the stump into a sandwich bag for later. (You'll recall the *Seinfeld* episode in which Elaine hatches a plan to sell only muffin tops, while unloading the stumps at a homeless shelter.)

The muffin has been sitting on the counter since August 26. Today is October 3. There's dust collecting on the sandwich bag, but the muffin inside is soft to the touch. Absolutely no sign of mold, either.

This got me wondering. What kind of surreal food preservatives are in this thing?

The FDA maintains a list of ingredients called *Everything Added to Food in the United States* (EAFUS), which lists more than 3,000 items.

Vitamins C and E are sometimes added to food products as a preservative. But the most popular chemical additives in the food industry today are benzoates, nitrites, sulphites, and sorbates. These additives kill and prevent molds and yeast from growing on food. Sulfur dioxide is the most common man-made preservative; it acts as a bleaching agent in food.

Most EAFUS ingredients are benign, but a few of them do have potentially harmful effects.

On the website "Eat This, Not That!" are listed the ten scariest food additives. Here are two that might be lurking in my zombie muffin stump.

- Azodicarbonamide, a synthetic yellow–orange dough conditioner, is used most frequently in the production of industrial foam plastic. In a review of forty-seven studies on azodicarbonamide, the World Health Organization concluded that it probably triggers asthma. The WHO concluded, "Exposure levels should be reduced as much as possible." This stuff is in Dunkin' Donuts bagels and McDonald's burger buns.
- Ammonium sulfate is an inorganic salt that occurs naturally near active volcanoes and is used commercially to nourish yeast and help bread rise. However, this compound is most often used as fertilizer—and in flame retardants. Both the Center for Science in the Public Interest and the FDA deem it safe, so you'll find it in Subway rolls, among other places.

This is a complicated and controversial subject, but food expert Michael Pollan makes it simple. He recommends that we avoid anything our great-grandparents would not recognize as food.

As for my lemon-poppy seed zombie, I'm with Stephen King, who says in *Pet Sematary*, "Sometimes dead is better."

# 67

## *Coat of Many Colors*

Even before the current controversy about immigrants, I'd been convinced that the United States should be thought of not as a melting pot but as a coat of many colors.

*The Melting Pot* was a 1908 play that popularized the idea of a fusion of different nationalities, ethnicities, and cultures into an ideal republic.

Modern sociologists have largely discarded the term. "Cultural pluralism" or "multiculturalism" are more to the point in describing the kind of assimilation we experience today, where immigrants are keen to retain their national cultures and ethnicities even as they take up residence in the United States.

The metaphor of "coat of many colors" comes from the Genesis story of Joseph. As told in the King James Version, Jacob "loved Joseph more than all his children, because he was the son of his old age: and he made him a coat of many colors."

Most coats worn in those days were functional—plain, knee-length, and short-sleeved to allow freedom of movement for work. But the coat Jacob gave his son was beautiful—colorful, ankle-length, and more in keeping with coats worn by those who did not work with their hands— nobility and royalty.

The coat of many colors symbolized favoritism. But that very favoritism by their father alienated Joseph from his brothers, who tried to do him in by selling him into slavery. The story has a happy ending, with Joseph eventually becoming governor of Egypt and reuniting with his father and brothers.

The story was popularized in *Joseph and the Amazing Technicolor Dreamcoat*, the first musical staged by Tim Rice and Andrew Lloyd Webber. It ran on Broadway in 1982–83 and also has seen more than twenty thousand school and amateur theater productions.

Country singer Dolly Parton, too, settled on the theme when she released her *Coat of Many Colors* album in 1971:

> *My coat of many colors that my momma made for me,*
> *Made only from rags but I wore it so proudly*

It is these words . . . "made only from rags" . . . that so closely describe the makeup of our nation.

So many of our immigrants—from Mayflower Puritans to Middle Eastern refugees—are ragged fragments torn from the whole cloth of the countries they fled.

And, like Joseph, the biblical shepherd who became a ruler, they are dreamers who settle on these shores to pursue dreams.

Former Vice President Hubert H. Humphrey, the commencement speaker at my Fordham graduation, isn't quoted very often. But, in my book, he did well with this thought:

> *It is the task of both the graduation class of 1965 and of our generation*
> *to convince the legislatures and the executives—not only of the United*
> *States but of Europe as well—that moral imperatives as well as physical*
> *security require a substantial commitment to long range economic and*

*technical assistance to the developing nations of the world. We must do this out of compassion—for we are our brother's keeper. And we must also do it out of self-interest as well—for our lot is their lot, our future their future, our peace their peace.*

# 68

## *Why So Lonely?*

By 2020, an entire generation will have grown up in a primarily digital world. Computers, Internet, mobile phones, social media—all are second nature to them. Along with this comes their unquenchable need for constant contact with large networks of persons. Generation C, some are already calling it ("C" for "connected"). Or should it be called The Lonely Generation?

Cisco estimates that by 2020, there will be fifty billion connected devices, with an accompanying 25 percent annualized decrease in price to connect.

This directly affects us here in North America, where right now nine of ten people are Internet users—the largest percentage in the world.

But there is another statistic we shouldn't overlook.

The National Science Foundation in 2014 reported that unprecedented numbers of Americans are lonely. One in four surveyed said they have no one with whom they can talk about their personal troubles or triumphs. If family members are not counted, the number doubles to more than half of Americans who have no one with whom to share confidences.

Why so lonely, then? Is The C Generation just a dispirited redux of the fifties Beat Generation?

Pope Francis, in his 2015 encyclical on the environment, warns that a person dominated by social media and the Internet risks substituting human relationships with virtual ones.

Social media, he writes, can shield us from direct contact with "the pain, the fears, and the joys of others and the complexity of their personal experiences." The abuse of the new media can cause "a deep and melancholic dissatisfaction with interpersonal relations, or a harmful sense of isolation."

The Pope's analysis echoes a number of psychologists and sociologists. For example, Dr. Jim Taylor, a psychologist and the author of *Raising Generation Tech*:

> *Research shows a significant decline in empathy and an increase in narcissism among young people compared to the previous generation. We can't determine whether the cause is social media and technology, but it's occurred pretty much coincidentally with the emergence of the Internet.*

Likewise, Dr. Alex Lickerman has called the Internet "an electronic drug that often yanks us away from the physical world." The problem, he says, "comes when we find ourselves subtly *substituting* electronic relationships for physical ones or mistaking our electronic relationships for physical ones. We may feel we're connecting effectively with others via the Internet, but too much electronic-relating paradoxically engenders a sense of social isolation."

Former presidential speechwriter Janice Shaw Crouse points out that, "In an era of instant communication . . . some would argue that it doesn't make sense that people are lonely. Nevertheless, sharing—the antidote to loneliness—is not the same thing as talking."

Rabbi Daniel Lapin has perhaps the most unsettling analysis, calling The C Generation "orphans in time."

Today's generation of young people, he says, is "incapable of integrating their past and their future . . . living instinctively in an almost animal-like fashion only in the present."

He notes that it is virtually impossible, then, to connect time and space in a way that enables them to build their "present." Thus, they wander aimlessly, without true connections—physically, emotionally, or spiritually.

# 69

## *The Right to Be Happy*

If life's purpose lies in getting what we want, as our culture insists, then freedom becomes a very big deal. Freedom is what allows us to exercise our "inalienable right" to the pursuit of happiness.

With this view of freedom, it's easy to feel threatened by constraint. Our instinct is to resist it with all our might, for it impedes our ability to live the life we want.

To maximize this kind of freedom requires that we minimize or even eliminate serious relationships. For the more we rely on others or others rely on us, the less free we are to go wherever we wish to go, pursue whatever we wish to pursue, and do whatever we wish to do.

The idea of loving someone unconditionally, without anticipating love or appreciation in return—constrains us. In a society devoted to self-fulfillment, the cost of love often seems too high.

We cling to emotions for happiness, such as feeling approval and affection. These are symbols of security that help us survive infancy and childhood. But they are inappropriate for adulthood because when we pursue them wholeheartedly we more often find frustration, anger, discouragement, panic, guilt, shame.

Paula Huston says in her book, *A Season of Mystery*, that in the Bible, the "free" person is the one no longer plagued by the burdensome quest for money, pleasure, possessions, social status, and political power. Interestingly, aren't these the same things that our culture says will fulfill us and make us happy?

When we adhere to the idea that "I have a right to be happy" we fool ourselves—at the cost of failed relationships, unprofitable ambitions, and unhappy lives.

Valuing ourselves only according to our successes, fame, or fortune causes us to miss the essential.

The way to inner contentment, Ms. Huston writes, is to value ourselves as the Divine does—simply for who we are.

# 70

## *Great Expectations*

I became a speechwriter for IBM instead of a college professor . . . while my friend Chet was laid off by IBM and became a college professor.

My second cousin, Dean, was working at a gym . . . where a chance conversation with a celebrity news anchor led to a career as a network TV producer.

At the age when most retire, the architect of my house found himself a hotelier . . . a new reason to keep building buildings.

Is it serendipity? Or our own openness to discern and exploit unexpected opportunity?

The ancients believed that three women controlled all human destiny. They called them The Fates, traditionally depicted in art and sculpture as weavers of a tapestry that dictated the destinies of us mortals.

My friend, Impressionist painter Ilona Royce Smithkin, is in her ninety-seventh year. "I never expect anything," she'll tell you, "so I'm never disappointed."

Saint Paul, too, advised against great expectations: "I have learned to be content in whatever state I am."

Yes, but.

It's also true that if beginning monks are going to abandon the monastic life, they usually do it during the few years after their solemn profession of vows. Why? They fall into the trap of thinking there are no new heights to achieve—no more great expectations.

When unanticipated events result in happy outcomes, we call it serendipity.

Perhaps the best-known example of serendipity is Alexander Fleming, who was working at a hospital in 1928 when he noticed that a culture of *staphylococcus aureus* had become contaminated with mold—and the mold was destroying the bacteria. This chance observation led to the development of penicillin and other antibiotics. X-rays, radiation, and pulsars, Velcro, Vaseline, and Teflon—all owe their existence to serendipity.

Can we make serendipity happen? Can we give life to our great expectations?

Dr. Stephann Makri of the University College London Interaction Centre says: "By looking for patterns in peoples' memorable examples of serendipity, we've found that it is more than just a 'happy accident.' It also involves insight—an 'aha' moment of realization."

In a paper titled, "Maximising Serendipity," James Lawley and Penny Tompkins describe six components that need to be in place for serendipity to occur:

- A prepared mind
- An unplanned and unexpected event
- A recognition of the potential for positive significance
- Action taken to amplify the potential for positive effect
- Effects of the action—which are utilized to further amplify the benefit
- Value of the original event and the subsequent effects becomes apparent—at which time serendipity can be said to have taken place.

Recognition and action. In other words, expect the unexpected, then jump on it with both feet.

Stand-up comic Steven Wright acknowledges: "You can't have everything. Where would you put it?" But you might get a bigger slice of life's pie—if you slice it yourself.

# 71

## *Anniversaries*

*A couple was celebratin' their fiftieth wedding anniversary with a reception. They were standin' in line greetin' their friends and about halfway through, she hauled off and hit him. He looked surprised and said, "What was that for?" She said, "For fifty years of bad sex!" He thought about that a minute and then hauled off and hit her. Now it was her turn to look surprised and she said, "What was that for?" He answered, "For knowing the difference!"*

**—MINNIE PEARL**

The earliest references to wedding anniversaries date from the 1800s. They seem to have originated in the Germanic region, where the custom was for the spouse to crown his wife with a silver garland when they had been married for twenty-five years. Gold became the second traditional anniversary crown, after fifty years.

These thoughts are on my mind because yesterday my wife, Jo Anne, and I have just marked our fiftieth wedding anniversary.

A widely quoted proverb says, "A society grows great when old men plant trees whose shade they know they shall never sit in." If we follow this line of thought, we might conceive of marriage as a tapestry woven not for ourselves, but as a benefaction for our children and grandchildren.

Jo Anne has been a golden thread in the tapestry of our long life together, giving it meaning and direction.

The symbolism of golden thread—spirituality and purity—fits her precisely. Viking housewives spun and wove all the cloth, and the spindle came to represent womanly wisdom, virtue, and industry. In the hands of *Frigg*, the Norse goddess, the spindle became strong magic. The kind of magic Jo Anne brought to our union.

In my Ukrainian religious tradition, the sacrament of marriage is acknowledged as a union, not a contract. No vows are made in our marriage ceremony.

A Ukrainian wedding, as in other Eastern churches, begins with the couple being "betrothed" with the exchange of rings. Prayers call on God to come into the lives of the couple and unite them in one mind and wed them in one flesh. A high point of the ritual comes when the priest places a crown on the heads of the bride and groom to signify the dawn of a new kingdom to be ruled by the couple—side by side.

For Jo Anne and me, fifty years later, the crowns might be a bit battered by the passing of decades, but the heartbeats are intensified. As novelist Radclyffe writes in *Love's Masquerade*: "When we follow the conventional milestones, meting out our lives with birthdays and graduations and anniversaries and funerals, we are left with voids along the way—vast stretches of empty space lost forever, never to be filled. As time grows short, the significance of each moment increases, until finally every heartbeat is of monumental importance."

# 72

## *Remember*

*My wife of fifty years died as dawn was breaking on December 1, 2015. I prepared this remembrance for the Mass of Christian Burial celebrated for her today:*

In 1963 I was studying at Fordham University during the day and working nights at the *New York Daily News*. I vividly remember the day I met Jo Anne in the student lounge. She tried to sell me tickets to the Glee Club concert. I turned her down.

That was probably the last time I said "no" to her.

I went to work that night and told a friend, "I just met the girl I'm going to marry."

We did marry. Last week Jo Anne and I renewed our vows in honor of our fiftieth wedding anniversary. Except this time we were not in a church . . . but in a hospital room.

The other day someone asked me about Jo Anne's career. I didn't know how to answer. She did so much: kindergarten teacher . . . owner of a dance studio . . . choreographer of musicals . . . producer of corporate events . . . a model . . . a painter . . . a voiceover narrator . . . a video editor.

As an actor she portrayed spirited characters like the foul-mouthed Gwen in Lanford Wilson's *Fifth of July* . . . the hungover hooker in Neil Simon's *California Suite* . . . Bob Cratchit's steadfast wife in *A Christmas Carol* . . . and, of course, she created the title role in the premiere of *Lady Kay*.

She was the golden thread in the fabric of my life. The golden girl whose life gave meaning and direction to mine.

She showed great love, to me and to so many others. That was her great gift to us.

When you've seen great love, you've seen the face of God . . . because God is love.

Maybe this was why she asked to have as her epitaph:

*"All I ask of you is forever to remember me as loving you."*

What I will always remember is her strength and encouragement when she whispered what would be some of her last words: "Life goes by in a flash; I'll see you in a few minutes."

# 73

## *Letter from the Desert*

With Hanukkah under way and Christmas around the corner, this doesn't seem a time to write about deserts. But when my wife of fifty years withdrew from this world last week, I found myself left in an abandoned place.

But is the desert such a poor place to be?

For Jesus, the desert was sanctuary: "Rising very early before dawn, he left and went off to a deserted place, where he prayed."

Several years ago Jo Anne and I visited the Sinai, where Moses discovered the bush that burns but is not turned to ash, where the soul can burst into flame with the fire of the Spirit and not be consumed—but cleansed.

In that desert, as medieval monk William of Saint-Thierry wrote, "The soul attains to the holy place where none may stand or take another step, except he be bare-footed, having loosed the shoestrings of all fleshly hindrances."

It is the desert, too, where writers and artists come to contend with the unseen.

Thomas Merton, for example. Although this Trappist monk and prolific writer would not see an actual desert until shortly before his death, he knew the desert as a symbolic landscape and had studied the early Christian hermits known today as the Desert Fathers.

In the years before Merton's literary flowering in the 1960s, he underwent a personal desert experience of anguish, anxiety, and depression. Merton scholar David D. Cooper noted that this period of withdrawal, solitude, alienation, and despair resulted in Merton's discovery of his "true self."

Merton, says Cooper, struggled to reconcile his vocation as a monk with his calling as a writer. He did not give up the desert struggle, and the result was that he "began to speak with the voice of prophetic and eschatological protest."

Gabriel García Márquez, the Colombian author of *One Hundred Years of Solitude*, noted the writer's need to slough off the immaterial: "To be a good writer you have to be absolutely lucid at every moment of writing." How better to find lucidity than in solitude?

From Moses to Merton to Márquez, the searing recognition of self and our place in the cosmos comes in solitude, in the purging cauldron of silence.

We might reside in a metropolis of millions, yet feel alone. Or, perhaps worse, we might dole out our days in a soulless relationship. In my case, with the "soul of the house" gone—*alma de casa* as the Spanish say—a quiet monotony threatens, like a creeping fog on a chill Cape Cod night.

But I remember that each of us carries poetry in our breast, and I write with increased industriousness, taking heart in Percy Bysshe Shelley's, "A poet is a nightingale, who sits in darkness and sings to cheer its own solitude with sweet sounds."

In doing so, I discover that the unfamiliar darkness left by my wife's departure has become yet another of her gifts to me.

# 74

## The Sinister Side of Christmas

We work so hard each December at making Christmas merry, but the roots of our celebrations run deep and dark.

Within the past several days, I've attended performances of Charles Dickens's *A Christmas Carol* on Cape Cod and George Balanchine's *The Nutcracker* at Lincoln Center. Two vastly different interpretations of the holiday, but they share a dark heritage.

In E. T. A. Hoffmann's 1816 story, "The Nutcracker and the Mouse King," on which the 1892 Tchaikovsky ballet is based, scary old Drosselmeyer was once the royal rat-catcher, who set traps for the Mouse Queen. This led to a series of incidents that ended in his nephew being turned by an evil spell into a nutcracker.

Hoffmann might have been rebelling against the Enlightenment and its emphasis on rational philosophy. As a Romantic, he believed that imagination was under attack by rationalism. His tale challenged readers to liberate their inner child from the monotony of the real world.

Hoffmann's Romantic approach to imagination, reality, and childhood has been lost in most productions of *The Nutcracker*. The ballet—saved only by Tchaikovsky's brilliant score—is a holiday diversion full of dancing and merriment. But there's nothing profound in its storyline.

Then there's Charles Dickens's *A Christmas Carol*. Today is the anniversary of its publication on December 19, 1843.

Most of us probably have never read the book, but we've all seen plenty of film or theatrical adaptations.

Have you noticed that Dickens leaves out Baby Jesus—and concentrates on grotesquery, poverty, indignity, pranks, dancing, food, and death?

There are thousands of novels that tell us we should be kinder and more moral, novelist Michel Faber says, but most of them gather dust. The secret of *A Christmas Carol* lies in the real reason for Scrooge's change of heart—his realization that, at long last, he's capable of having fun.

Like Hoffmann's Romantic view of what life can be, the greatest tragedy Dickens can imagine is an existence devoid of playfulness, of biding time on the way to the grave. Fun, for him, is the only redress for death. Scrooge's triumph is that he looks his own corpse in the face and defiantly resolves to enjoy the gift of life to the full.

It's not hard to figure out why Christmas fables like *A Christmas Carol* and *The Nutcracker* draw on the somber to set things in motion. After all, the biblical narrative of the Nativity has its own sinister backstory, with evil Herod conniving to learn the location of the would-be king of the Jews so he can assassinate the infant in his crib. Failing that, he orders the massacre of every Hebrew boy under the age of two:

*"A voice was heard in Ramah, sobbing and loud lamentation; Rachel weeping for her children, and she would not be consoled, since they were no more."*

But true to the manner of Hoffmann and Dickens, at this time of good cheer we might do well to declare death null and void in favor of living a full and loving life, one in which we are, at long last, capable of having fun.

# 75

## Scrooge Is Alive and Well
## and Living in Silicon Valley

According to the famous first line of Dickens's *A Christmas Carol*, "Marley was dead."

Marley may be dead. But Scrooge still lives.

My friend, and a former journalist, Charles Paolino, points out that, "The key to Dickens's thinking is in Scrooge's conversation with Marley's Ghost, specifically Marley's lament that during his lifetime he had not allowed his spirit to go out among his fellow human beings, and that in death he was condemned to travel endlessly, observing the pain and want that he no longer has the power to assuage."

Fast-forward 173 years since Dickens published his novella, and "observe the pain" that seemingly civilized, sensitive authority figures impose on their subordinates.

I write this post after a conversation with a client who was fired from her ranking managerial job at a global company headquartered in Silicon

Valley. A company that's a household name, that claims it is the underpinning of the entire Internet.

Her dismissal came during the celebratory days of Hanukkah—and a week before Christmas.

My client was a top performer who hit it out of the park every at-bat. The bosses called their action "lay off," which holds out the tenuous hope of being welcomed back at some future better time when business is better. But everybody knows the phrase has become a lame euphemism for "fired." Just as sure as we know men don't patronize Hooters for the hamburgers.

Meanwhile, subordinates on her team who were already under review for poor performance at the time of the "lay off" are still working.

She was making too much money.

What about pay for performance and motivating employees toward loyalty? What is an employee to deduce when his or her manager is fired because the manager earns too much?

What about the concept of apprenticeship, of younger employees learning from the experience and wisdom of senior people?

What about the corporation's investment in the intellectual capital of its senior leadership?

What about the milk of human kindness?

When I was a manager at IBM and then at Siemens, a significant part of my responsibility was to recruit people for career employment. We hired people for a career, not just a job.

Candidates were not interviewed by six, eight, or ten people. I hired directly, with the approval of only my immediate manager. The human resources department took care of the paperwork. The result of this approach? IBM during my twenty-year tenure was known as the best-managed company in the world.

My client's Silicon Valley company is not unique. The practice of jettisoning high-salaried employees seems ubiquitous in corporate America.

They don't heed Marley's warning. But they do follow Scrooge's—to "decrease the surplus population."

# 76

## *Exits and Entrances*

At year's end it's customary to look back to review while looking forward to renew. It's a time of transition, when a new portal opens to us to either pass through to a new beginning—or cling to a past that cannot return.

This is why ancient Romans built their cardinal temple to Janus with one door facing the rising sun and the other its setting.

The familiar, two-headed likeness of Janus crowned the doorways of many Roman residences. His name, in fact, was taken from the Etruscan word *jauna,* which means "door."

Janus was thought of as the Porter of Heaven and invoked at the start of each day. This Guardian of Exits and Entrances symbolized both beginning and end. He was supreme gatekeeper, presiding over the start of all activities. He inaugurated the seasons. The first day of each month was his holy day. He served as a constant reminder that we must pass through a portal in order to enter a new place. Deference was paid to him at life's most important beginnings, such as birth and marriage.

That's why I've been thinking about Janus lately. Because on December 1, 2015, my companion for most of my life died.

When my wife transitioned from this life to what we trust will be her next, she passed through the portal alone, thereby presenting me with a portal of my own.

In her book, *Uncoupling: Turning Points in Intimate Relationships*, Diane Vaughan described the phenomenon this way:

*Uncoupling is a transition into a different lifestyle, a change of life course which, whether we recognize and admit it in the early phases or not, is going to be made without the other person.*

We might better understand life's transitions if we think of a portal not only as a door, but also as a choice. A choice between potential and act, stasis and motion.

The choice I face as I enter a new stage of my life, of being "single" again, is whether to enlarge my life by embracing new possibilities offered by a changed lifestyle or watch myself lessen through self-indulgent inertia.

The nature of life is change. The ancient Romans recognized this fact when they created their god of transitions. The nature of human beings, on the other hand, is to resist change.

Elizabeth Lesser, author of *Broken Open: How Difficult Times Can Help Us Grow*, puts it so well: "How ironic that the difficult times we fear might ruin us are the very ones that can break us open and help us blossom into who we were meant to be."

The choice I face as I enter the new year of 2016 is one that none of us welcomes, but one that each of us must make in times of unwelcome transition. We must choose between the rising of the sun and its setting.

# 77

## *Slack Tide*

Life is a blur of information, obligations, and commitments. So what else is new? But at midnight on New Year's—as at no other moment of the year—both hands of the clock pause and join to point heavenward in the classic pose of prayer.

In oceanography, slack tide is the imperceptible, discreet moment when the tide pauses—and turns. Midnight is the slack tide of our day; New Year's the slack tide of the year. And each of us has one particular day that is the slack tide of our life.

When we reach our forties, some corporeal switch turns on and reverses our body's growth. It's the slack tide of our life, when old age commences, no matter what we do to avoid it. Hair whitens. Skin sags. Libido begs off. We start shutting down, cell by cell, in our inevitable descent toward decay.

When we're twenty we look out over the next forty years and think, "I can make anything of my life that I want." We expect the unexpected. We anticipate that anything can happen. But, come forty, we pretty much know what the remnant is. At forty, the mystery is gone. Sad to say, life mandates mystery if it's to be fully lived.

Our personal Slack Day ought to be observed, don't you think, with an event of some formality, like a birthday? A party is in order. Gifts from friends and singing around a cake. One's Slack Day is much more important than one's birthday. A birthday is backward-looking. Slack Day forces our focus forward, even if it is to face our decline.

When we can for a moment avoid the stresses of information, obligations, and commitments, we can summon up a kind of slack tide for our psyche. There is a pause. Everything hesitates. We can take a deep breath.

Like a mini-New Year, we can free ourselves for a slice of time so we can think about ourselves and our desire to be better, to be all we believe we can be or want to be. To make resolutions.

This is the idea of going on a spiritual "retreat." Retreats are an integral part of many Hindu, Buddhist, Catholic, and Sufi faith traditions. A "rainy-season" retreat, for example, was the ancient custom of South Asian ascetics when they would retire to a forest grove for the duration of the monsoon. Jesus set a model by fasting in the desert for forty solitary days. Lent, Yom Kippur, Ramadan—all are times when practitioners enter a calming state of separation, of repentance, resolution, and renewal.

There are more than 2,500 retreat centers of various kinds around the world. It seems that the more wired we are, the more appealing being "unwired" becomes.

It's fitting for us in the Northern Hemisphere that New Year's comes during winter. Because even with its storms, winter is the quietest time of year. There is nothing like the quiet after a storm. Here on Outer Cape Cod, I can stand out on my deck and hear only the wind. I can walk on the beach and see only shorebirds and seals.

It is in such stillness that we hear what God hears.

# 78

## *What We Learn from Turtles*

Cape Cod, where I live, stretches 70 miles into the Atlantic Ocean, surrounded by Cape Cod Bay on the north, Buzzards Bay on the west, Vineyard and Nantucket sounds on the south, and the Atlantic Ocean on the east. Sea turtles love our bay about as much as I do. Each spring, they work their way north from the Caribbean for summertime feeding.

But the outstretched arm of Cape Cod acts as a giant seine that catches them in a death embrace.

So while you and I were supping on roasted goose and flaming plum pudding this Christmas, Massachusetts Audubon Society volunteers were patrolling the beaches near my home. They rescued close to five hundred "cold-stunned" sea turtles that were washed ashore by strong December winds.

The majority of these Cheloniidae were Kemp's ridley turtles, a critically endangered species and the rarest of all sea turtles. Most of those that washed ashore would have died except for the unseasonably warm temperatures this year. And volunteer rescuers like my daughter, Julie.

As autumn sets in, too many turtles linger too long, misled by the comfort of the bay's warm, shallow waters. Oblivious to the approaching winter, they miss their chance to swim for the open ocean—and safe passage south. Not only that, their instincts drive them southward when autumn approaches. They should be heading, instead, north and then east to clear the clenched fist of Provincetown.

For a long time, I've thought about the parallel between the numbed turtles' plight and the paralysis many of us suffer when we wake too late to a lifetime best described as unnoticed.

Zora Neale Hurston, the noted Harlem Renaissance author of the 1920s, captured what I mean:

*You don't take no steps at all, just stand around and hope for things to happen outright, unthankful and unknowing, like a hog under an acorn tree, eating, grunting, with your ears hanging over your eyes and never even looking up to see where the acorns are coming from.*

What can we learn from turtles? Here's how I write about it in my novel, *Little Flower: A Killing on Cape Cod.*

*Hers was the paralysis of the ridleys on the winter beach, cold-stunned. She felt that she had been wandering without destination in an enveloping fog, like the thick fumes that lift off the Bay on winter mornings. She was confused about which direction to turn, not knowing what to do to save the remains of her life, and running out of energy to do anything, like a car left parked with its headlights on. It was not her husband who had become a stranger to her. It was herself that she no longer knew. Everything was coming home to roost. Her role in the near-euthanasia of her mother. Her refusal to confront her father for his abhorrent abuse. Her capitulation to Eater. Even her career, launched by theft and fueled by sexual dabbling.*

*Jenny was not surprised to see the turtle's carcass ahead. It was without predator damage, or decay. The gulls hadn't found it yet, perhaps because the ebbing tide had left it behind only moments ago. Jenny sat on the damp sand several feet from the turtle and crossed her legs. She now knew that any decision she made would entail confrontation— with Eater, with Ryan, with herself. Like the ridleys, she would have to betray her instincts in order to escape.*

# 79

## *Fear Is a Color*

In January 2014, Pope Francis was speaking to the throng gathered in the piazza below his window. He appealed for peace in Ukraine, where recent demonstrations against government corruption had resulted in the death of protesters.

He chose to close his message in a picturesque way—by having two doves released from the window. But the gesture was memorable in a way Francis never anticipated.

The doves were immediately attacked by a crow and a seagull. Feathers flew, but we never learned what ultimately happened to the doves.

The Pope might have gotten the ill-fated dove idea from the Gospel depiction of Christ's baptism in the Jordan River by his cousin, now known as Saint John the Baptist. Witnesses spoke of seeing a dove hover overhead and hearing a disembodied voice say, "You are my beloved son, in whom I am well pleased."

George W. Rutler, author and pastor of Saint Michael's church in the Hell's Kitchen neighborhood of Manhattan, explains:

*The Holy Spirit came down on Christ 'like a dove.' Artists portray this as best they can, but one can get the impression that the Holy Spirit actually was a bird.*

I'm not writing about all this because I am of Ukrainian ancestry, but because the incident in Rome was iconic of the seemingly eternal victimization of weakness by strength, of innocence by evil, of resolve by temptation.

The attack on the doves was worthy of an Alfred Hitchcock treatment. But the story needs no fictionalization. It is too true.

How could Hitchcock conjure up a more inhuman image than the young Syrian jihadist who early this month murdered his mother in a public square while hundreds watched? He performed that act scant days before Catholics around the world celebrated the Baptism of Jesus.

Reverend Rutler says, "Baptism begins a fight."

It was after his baptism, remember, that Jesus went into the desert to do battle with his great tempter, Satan.

And Saint John the Baptist told the crowds that, "one mightier than I is coming who will baptize you with the Holy Spirit and with fire."

With fire.

Saint Bernard said as long ago as the twelfth century: "Fear is a color. As soon as it touches our liberty, it stains it."

Perhaps this is why good people flee. Because they recognize evil as something subhuman. Something beneath them. Perhaps they flee not so much to find sanctuary as to assert the humanity of us all.

# 80

## *A Stinker of a Business Lesson*

The original *Star Wars* was the perfect movie—fast, funny, filled with characters who were a hoot.

The new version left me astoundingly disappointed. It's a stinker.

This film simply updated the original's storyboards with new faces and new dialog. The storyline was practically the same, right down to everybody chasing after the dopey little droid.

In the new version, Darth Vader has been replaced by a pale geek we're asked to believe is his grandson. In lieu of Luke Skywalker is an actress not as likable as Mark Hamill and not as pretty as Natalie Portman. And where the young Han Solo strode the galaxy with his devilishly devastating smirk is a dweeby stand-in who is a short suit both as character and actor.

The proof rests in the fact that I left the cinema unable to remember the name of even one of the new characters.

But I wanted to know why movies like this are successful. So I did a bit of reading about the film industry. Here's what I found:

- The six major Hollywood studios have been around for a century, making this arguably the most stable business in US history.
- Studios spend less money on making films than they do marketing them around the world—with most of the revenue generated not in theater showings but in home video and sales to television.
- Because they mostly turn out movies costing more than three hundred million dollars each, studios mostly stick to what's worked before.

Key, however, is that Hollywood has a knack for identifying who their audience is—and getting a pulse on that audience's interests. The daughter who dragged me to see the new *Star Wars* adored it, for instance, because she grew up with the franchise and felt "at home."

Like the Distant Early Warning radar network of the Cold War era—known as the DEW Line—the studios identify audience interests before the rest of us do.

I like to think of myself as a lifelong learner, so I asked myself what I could learn from this stinker of a movie that I might apply to my own corporate communications practice and to my fiction and nonfiction writing.

And it's this:

First, never lose sight of fundamentals. In resurrecting the *Star Wars* franchise, Disney went back to the original and came up with something that's shattering every industry record.

Second, build your own DEW Line. So you can be ahead of the pack in recognizing what's about to come thundering at you from over the horizon—and be quick and bold in adapting.

Finally maintain your motivation. The way to do that is by going out every day and proving you're the best at what you do, as Disney has done since you and I were kids.

# 81

## *The Hardest Love*

I've been devastatingly hurt by someone I trusted completely.
Who hasn't?

This is why, with Saint Valentine's Day coming up tomorrow, I'm writing about a different manifestation of love that we don't talk about very much because it's the hardest love—forgiveness.

Every world religion or philosophy encourages forgiveness, from Confucianism to Wicca.

But most of us don't recognize forgiveness as an act of love. Or we don't buy it. Or we make our forgiveness contingent on our betrayer's remorse.

I use the word betray intentionally. To betray is to act in the interest of the enemy.

French philosopher Jacques Derrida suggests that the more unforgivable the act, the greater the call to forgive.

Philosopher Lucy Allais of the University of California, says that when someone does us wrong, our perception of that person is altered for the worse, usually irrevocably. We judge that the person has failed us dramatically, and we feel deep—and justifiable—resentment.

Sometimes we excuse, justify, or accept the betrayal, which amounts to saying there is really nothing to forgive, that it "wasn't your fault." This is not forgiveness, Dr. Allais says.

Nor is saying, "I forgive but I won't forget." This is an admission that our love has strings attached, that I will love you only if you are deserving. This kind of faux forgiveness condemns us to seeing our hurt and resentment return again and again.

Wholehearted forgiveness requires that we overcome the resentment we're entitled to and see the person the way we did prior to their wrongdoing.

We're not required to forgive. It's discretionary. It's a decision. But feelings and emotions can't be changed by a simple act of will, especially when our instincts are raging for revenge.

Nor is forgiveness meant to be therapy for the forgiver, despite what we hear about resentment being as destructive as holding a burning coal in our hand.

Rather, when we forgive, we enlarge our hearts.

How? Because we are bestowing on our betrayer more than their due, more than their actions warrant—whether they express remorse or not. And this can be immensely empowering to one who forgives.

My own motivation to forgive can be found in words written by author Elizabeth Lowell: "I'm not perfect. Remember that, and try to forgive me when I fail you."

Or Mother Teresa's: "Self-knowledge sends us to our knees."

Maybe this is what Pope Francis meant with his famous: "Who am I to judge?"

The ancient Greeks coined four words for love: *storge*, the affection we have for family members; *philia*, the bond between friends; *eros*, the desire for physical union; and *agape*, our unselfish willingness to sacrifice for the sake of another.

Theologian Reinhold Niebuhr picked up where they left off and defined forgiveness as "the final form of love."

It's the form of love the Greeks failed to name.

# 82

## *Going It Alone*

My house rests silent at dusk. Dresses crowd one another in her closet, the scent of perfume still lingering on them months after her departure. In the kitchen, a cold stove. These all gang up against me as afternoons end. It's called loneliness.

We all fear loneliness, whether caused by the rupture of a relationship, a divorce, a death. Still others admit to loneliness even while sharing a household.

But there is a way out of this unhappiness, I'm finding. By journeying inward.

Blaise Pascal, in his *Pensées*, put his finger on it: "Our unhappiness arises from one thing only, that we cannot be comfortably alone in our room."

One of the Himalayan masters defines the lonely person as one dependent on externals—persons or things—without awareness of the reality within. "Seek within," he urges, "to become aware that you are complete in yourself. God gave you a perfect soul. You don't need externals. No matter what happens in any situation, you need never be lonely."

This search to see our true self—not the two-dimensional self we see through the eyes of other people—can be done only in solitude:

*You must have a room, or a certain hour or so a day, where you don't know what was in the newspapers that morning, you don't know who your friends are, you don't know what you owe anybody, you don't know what anybody owes you. This is a place where you can simply experience and bring forth what you are and what you might be.*

—**JOSEPH CAMPBELL,** *THE POWER OF MYTH*

Solitude engenders an interior conversation that leads to self-discovery, to creativity, to authenticity.

Every religious tradition—and most philosophical schools—advise us to draw within and separate ourselves from the world in order to achieve inner peace and insight.

Solitude is something we choose, and we create it whenever or wherever we like.

We can be alone, but we are not in solitude if we are reading, studying, or absorbed in an iPhone. On the other hand, we can be in a crowd and wrap ourselves in solitude.

In other words, by choosing solitude we don't simply withdraw from society. We transcend it. Solitude is more than being alone. It's an active experience in which we still the mind.

We obviously cannot be in solitude all the time. We have to balance solitude and society.

Thoreau, for example, bragged about solitude as his "companion" but left Walden each week to have dinner with his mother. Socrates still holds the solitude record, I think. They say he once stood for twenty-four hours—thinking.

Montaigne suggested that our mind needs a "back shop" where we go for solitude. These periods of solitude prepare us for healthy participation in society. He spent hours in his library "conversing" with the great minds of the past through books. Then he would spend time in solitude, holding an interior conversation with himself.

Perhaps Montaigne got the idea from Jesus, who advised his followers: "But when you pray, go to your inner room, close the door, and pray to your Father in secret."

That inner room is in our hearts, where Jesus promised we would find God. We might also find ourselves there.

# 83

## *Succubus on My Chest*

I have forgiven and try to forget, but my mind betrays me with imagined scenarios of the iniquity that went on behind my back. And when my harrowing dreams wake me in the night, I wake to the thought of the betrayal—riding my chest like a succubus.

This is the dispiriting aspect of forgiveness—to forgive is a decision of the will, to forget is beyond our control. The pain of remembering revisits again and again, like an untreated abscess.

Aristotle taught that the best kind of friendship is that in which we see ourself in our friend.

But sometimes things like the following happen, as depicted in the recent movie, *45 Years*. The couple approaching this milestone wedding anniversary have this revelatory exchange:

> *Geoff Mercer: You really believe you haven't been enough for me?*
> *Kate Mercer: No. I think I was enough for you. I'm just not sure you do.*

This is why it hurts so much when we discover we didn't know our friend at all. It leads us to suspect we don't know ourselves either.

Why am I writing about this? Because of a conversation last week with a friend who has suffered a betrayal: "I had an epiphany. I've realized that I need to forgive myself."

This comment deserves to be shared, because there are vast numbers of us who take the blame for things not our fault.

When someone close fails us, we feel deep—and justifiable—hurt and resentment. Next, we ask why. Why was I betrayed? It must have been something I did. Or didn't do. Whichever, my own shortcoming caused the other person to wrong me. I drove them to it!

Is this a case of taking mature responsibility—which appears to be better than blaming our woes on everyone and everything else—or are we indulging in blame that's directed inward?

Our next thought? I must be a failure as a human being. And this translates to "I am unlovable." Dr. Craig Malkin asserts that we inevitably turn to self-doubt when we're afraid we can't control our experience.

Author Mike Robbins offers a cure:

*Letting go of blame allows us to be free, to take back our power and to avoid the trap of thinking that someone or something else has the ability to dictate our experience of life. Whether our life is "wonderful" or "difficult" is always up to us.*

Eleanor Roosevelt, whose personal life suffered a healthy portion of psychic insults, said, "No one can make you feel inferior without your consent."

The elixir of self-forgiveness, however, can be administered only if we step up to the fact that we are lovable, valuable, and singular.

"There is no love without forgiveness, and there is no forgiveness without love," says author Bryant H. McGill.

"Never forget to be compassionate to yourself," neurologist Debasish Mridha cautions. Because "to forgive others, you must forgive yourself first."

This idea is thought to stretch back to Hippocrates, he of the Hippocratic Oath.

The ancient Romans made it a proverb: *Medice, cura te ipsum.*

Even Christ quoted it in dealing with the Pharisees.

"Physician, heal thyself."

# 84

## *Best Friends*

For fifty years I never referred to my wife as my best friend. I thought it was an odd phrasing to apply to a spouse. "Friends" were Vic and Chuck and Bill. My wife was, well—my wife. A connection beyond friendship.

Now, in the aftermath of her death, I realize that our marriage endured for a half century precisely because she was my best friend.

In meditating about her passing, I've come to see that friendship is like holding a bird in your hand. Squeeze too tightly and you will smother it. Pay it too little heed and it will fly away.

Writer Simone de Beauvoir asks:

*Why one man rather than another? It was odd. You find yourself involved with a fellow for life just because he was the one that you met when you were nineteen.*

Jo Anne was nineteen when we met, both of us students at Fordham University. And, for better or worse, she found herself involved with me for life.

There also is something else that has me thinking about friendship—the four retired guys who meet for lunch every day at the Silver Star Diner down Second Avenue from Sloan-Kettering Memorial Cancer Center. Jo Anne and I would grab a meal there whenever she had the medical treatments that hopefully would contain her breast cancer. Every time we went to the Silver Star, they were there. Each of the old geezers was escorted by a paid caretaker, and the ladies would sit at a nearby table with a watchful eye on their decrepit charges, who indulged themselves with blini and sour cream.

I envy those guys. Because I would be hard pressed today to think of three men I could meet for lunch every day. Or even once a month.

So now, with my best friend gone, where do I find friendship?

Writing in *New York* magazine, Ann Friedman nicely summed up the problem for men: "They feel weird pursuing other men for friendship, or opening up to even those they considered pretty close friends."

Perhaps this is why men's friendships are often based on shared activities—playing golf, going to football games, working together on projects.

So I'm odd man out again. I think golf is stupid . . . football is dominated by domestic abusers . . . and I don't do "projects."

Dr. Ronald E. Riggio recently reported on a study that found women *court* their friends—with regular phone calls, for instance, and frequent get-togethers. Men, on the other hand, don't need to stay in touch. The research discovered that some men hadn't contacted "close" friends for many years. In a few cases, the close friend had passed away unbeknownst to the friend!

Which reminds me of the story of the four guys who got together to play eighteen holes of golf one afternoon. When they returned home, the wife of one of them asked, "How was the golf?"

"Great," her husband said. "Except on the sixth hole, Charlie had a heart attack and died."

"How terrible!" the wife exclaimed.

"It sure was," her husband replied, pulling a cold beer from the fridge. "All afternoon it was hit the ball, drag Charlie . . . hit the ball, drag Charlie."

# 85

## *From Darkness, Light*

Last weekend was the most wrenching I've experienced in a long
time. Blame it on a somber film about concealed sexual preda-
tion. And a day spent immersed in the cadences of a thousand men
praying.

It began with my viewing of *Spotlight*, the Oscar-winning film about
the sexual abuse scandal that has defined the Catholic Church in the
eyes of so many since the *Boston Globe* report in 2002.

Minutes into the movie, I set my popcorn aside and sat in the dark
cinema feeling shamed yet again by this never-ending story.

All I could think of was those pained and ruined boys and girls—
some gone from us by suicide—who in their hearts are singing the well-
known lines from "Over the Rainbow:"

*Someday I'll wish upon a star*
*And wake up where the clouds are far behind me.*
*Where troubles melt like lemon drops,*

217

*Away above the chimney tops,*
*That's where you'll find me.*

During the same weekend, however, I also attended an all-day conference for Catholic men in Worcester, Massachusetts. Similar events are held for women, but at this one were more than a thousand men of every age—many with teenaged sons in tow. No revival tent antics, but a day spent in prayerful reflection on topics ranging from spirituality to fatherhood.

I came away feeling heartened and hopeful to see so many ordinary "guys" fiercely intent on renewing their faith personally and restoring it institutionally.

These energized men encouraged me to think that perhaps the darkness that has enveloped my church might be giving way to the promise of light.

Can men like these end our recurring nightmare?

Who's to say?

After all, it was in total darkness that the God of Genesis commanded, "Let there be light."

He chose not to destroy darkness. He made it give way to the light.

As C. S. Lewis noted, "You never know how much you really believe anything until its truth or falsehood becomes a matter of life and death to you."

I found the truth of this right in my family.

Mine is an extended family of ethnicities and faiths, as our names suggest: Yaremko, Caruso, Debany, Selikowitz, LoGiudice, Sicoli, Kazanchi, Thyne, Schmitt.

We've suffered a number of deaths in recent years, most recently that of my wife three months ago. A curtain of darkness certainly has descended upon us.

But here, too, darkness is yielding to light.

Emily, the youngest mother in our family, gave birth two years ago to handsome Joseph. And two weeks ago, she brought shiny new Kayla into our world.

Oddly, our society makes more of a fuss about death than we do about birth—about the end of life rather than its beginning. We seem to think about people only when they die.

There's an old saying that, "When you were born, you cried and the world rejoiced. Live your life in such a way that when you die, the world cries and you rejoice."

# 86

## *"I Wish to Die for That Man"*

The crocuses poking through the last of the snow, the first golden blooms of forsythia, the imminent celebration of new life known as Easter—none of it kept my wife's close cousin from death a week ago. Cancer overwhelmed Robin Sicoli, just as it had my wife three months ago.

I drove the more than three hundred miles from Cape Cod to New Jersey for Robin's funeral in Berkeley Heights, one of the prettier places in the Garden State.

I was heading west along Route 78 when I saw the first forsythias of the new spring.

And it was in the face of Robin's passing—so closely after the death of my wife—that I renewed my hope.

I say that "I renewed" my hope, because hope—like faith and like love—is an act of the will.

This was convincingly demonstrated by Reverend Maximilian Kolbe, whom the Catholic Church considers a saint.

Because of his efforts to protect Jewish refugees, Kolbe was targeted by the Nazis, arrested, and sent to Auschwitz in 1941.

When one of the prisoners escaped, the guards decided to retaliate by starving ten of his fellow inmates to death.

One of the men chosen by the guards to die cried out, "My poor wife and children! I will never see them again!"

Kolbe stepped forward.

"I wish to die for that man," he announced to the guards.

And he did.

Viktor Frankl, the Austrian neurologist and psychiatrist who gained celebrity for the way in which he survived Auschwitz, brought scientific analysis to the idea of hope.

In his book, *Man's Search for Meaning*, Frankl points out that people in the horrible circumstances of the Nazi camps reacted in radically different ways. Some killed themselves. Others praised God even as they walked into certain death. He quoted Nietzsche's *Twilight of the Gods*: "He who has a *why* to live can bear with almost any *how*."

Hope has had many definitions through the ages.

Aristotle called hope "the dream of a waking man."

The thirteenth-century theologian, Thomas Aquinas, said that faith has to do with things that are not seen, while hope has to do with things that are not at hand.

Gabriel Marcel, who died in 1973, was a French philosopher, playwright, and musician. He explained hope this way:

*The essence of hope is not 'to hope that . . ." but merely 'to hope.' The person who hopes does not accept the current situation as final.*

Kolbe's ultimate self-sacrifice and Frankl's first-hand study underscore the idea that we need a hope that goes further than merely fulfilling career or lifestyle goals.

Hope—trust in the beyond—enables us truly to live.

# 87

## *Dueling with Ghosts*

I'm nearing the conclusion of Shirley Jackson's classic horror novel, *The Haunting of Hill House*, so ghosts must be on my mind these days. Of course, it doesn't help that I'm reading this book in bed to help me fall sleep.

This might explain why, as I was just awakening in the pre-dawn dark the other morning, a searing thought came from nowhere: "I'm dueling with ghosts."

A psychotherapist might disagree, but I don't think I'm alone in fighting phantasms of my own conjuring.

For example, why do I continue to hold grudges—for decades—against people who wronged me? Like that boss at IBM who held me back from promotion at a critical time in my career thirty years ago.

Against whom am I continuously competing? Why—when it comes to my particular area of expertise—do I need to be best?

Why do I continue to care how others judge me? Since I was a child,

I've had the vague feeling that I am being watched and weighed whenever I leave the house—whether I'm on the street, at a social gathering, even in church.

And what about jealousy? When will I get over my jealousy of Mr. Blue Eyes, whom my own wife couldn't take her eyes off?

How long will it take me to wholeheartedly forgive an intimate friend's infidelity and thereby heal my hurt?

All these ghosts feed on fear.

Ancient Chinese philosopher Lao Tzu is credited with saying, "There is no illusion greater than fear."

Watch a bird approach a birdbath. It moves in quick, nervous anticipation of danger. It jerks its head to look up, around and behind. Anything out of the ordinary and in a blink it beats its way to a high branch. Instinct warns the bird that with its beak and its gaze down to the water, it is vulnerable.

When our prehistoric ancestors dwelled on the plains of Africa, they must have been—like the bird—ceaselessly on the lookout for danger to their person or attack on their territory.

We still harbor these instincts deep within, I think. Why else do we need to control everything in our purview—from our health and safety to our work to our social and romantic relationships to our idea of self?

Even in our relationship with our creator, surrendering our will to his seems an insurmountable endeavor.

The author of the young-adult novel series, *Anne of Green Gables*, captured what I'm trying to say. Here is Lucy Maud Montgomery, writing in her 1926 novel, *The Blue Castle*. See if it doesn't speak to you, as it does to me:

> *"Fear is the original sin," suddenly said a still, small voice away back—back—back of Valancy's consciousness.*
>
> *"Almost all the evil in the world has its origin in the fact that some one is afraid of something."*
>
> *Valancy stood up. She was still in the clutches of fear, but her soul was her own again. She would not be false to that inner voice."*

Fear is a "cold, slimy serpent coiling about you," Ms. Montgomery wrote. And like any lethal serpent, it must be slain.

So, yes. In a way, I am dueling with ghosts. Maybe I always will.

# 88

## *Soufflé, Testosterone, and I*

A lot of guys read recipes the way they read science fiction. They get to the end and think, "Well, that's never going to happen."

It shouldn't be that way. If real men eat quiche, they can serve up soufflé, too.

It was the eminent James Beard who said, "The only thing that will make a soufflé fall is if it knows you're afraid of it."

Cooking is a primal act. Scientists believe that cooking helped develop the large human brain. The body absorbs significantly more energy from cooked meat, and processes it much more efficiently. This enabled extra energy to be used to develop the brain and cave paintings and music and dance and language.

Cooking is what separates us from the rest of the animals. Cooking also can separate valiant men who can make soufflé from those who are merely testosterone-glutted.

So why do many otherwise manly men fade at the thought of commanding a kitchen?

I'm not referring to professional chefs, such an overwhelmingly male profession that women have to work doubly hard to prove themselves. I'm talking about regular, run-of-the-mill guys. The ones who consider an electric blender a power tool, who can't tell cumin from cucumber, who truly believe that a watched pot won't boil.

It was my late wife who left me the gift of being comfortable in the kitchen. She convinced me of two things:

- Cooking—and especially baking—is a science. All you have to do is follow the instructions.
- Don't be afraid!

Here's Julia Child: "The only real stumbling block is fear of failure. In cooking you've got to have a what-the-hell attitude."

When I first started cooking, there was a ton of trial and error on my part. But eventually things clicked. Guests at my Vieques B&B started taking iPhone pictures of my breakfasts. At Christmas, I turned out a perfectly delicious leg of lamb for my visiting family's dinner.

It culminated two weeks ago when I invited two friends, who are also big-time foodies, for Sunday brunch.

After the Prosecco mimosas and fruit plate, I served a simple romaine salad dressed with a recipe from *The New York Times*, a soufflé I made from a recipe my wife had taught me, and the cranberry-walnut-orange sweet bread I serve at my Vieques bed-and-breakfast.

They asked for the bread recipe. Enough said.

Maybe I like cooking because it's like writing. No one enters the world a great writer or a great cook. You learn your craft by practicing it. Then science becomes art.

Also, no one writes or cooks alone. Even though you may be alone in your writing shack or your kitchen, you keep company with the practitioners of your craft who have gone before. As Laurie Colwin, a winner of the James Beard Award for Writing and Literature, wrote: "A cook in the kitchen is surrounded by generations of cooks past, the advice and menus of cooks present, the wisdom of cookbook writers."

# 89

## *The Good that I Would*

One of the most popular features in *The New York Times* is called "Sunday Routine." Each Sunday, the paper details the hour-by-hour activities that describe how a celebrity typically spends the day of rest.

It's the first feature I turn to, even though the featured persons are uniformly and vomit-inducingly pretentious.

Without fail, each will own a captivating dog or cat, clever children in private school, a fetching and equally successful spouse or partner, brunches at little-known but marvelous neighborhood restaurants, followed toward evening by dinners with fascinating friends.

I am much more interested to know about the daily routines of regular people—like me.

Because as an entrepreneur who makes his own schedule, I have been unable—for the life of me—to follow a routine.

Believe me, I've tried. I have read numerous books and articles on the subject. I have tried to imitate and emulate high achievers who seem to have it together. I have created template after template of a possible pattern for my day. Each seems wonderfully workable on paper. But when I put the plan into motion the next day? Poof!

Where I fail is in my lack of discipline in adhering to any of the routines I plan for myself.

I've read, for instance, that certain leaders—Pope Francis, for one—may rise as early as four in the morning to be productive or meditative during predawn's dark quiet.

So I set my alarm for four. But when the alarm jolts me awake, I acknowledge that this is a ridiculous idea, and I continue abed.

I am at my most creative in the morning, so I decide to start my day's writing with my first cup of coffee. But morning comes and I find myself doing a "quick" check of e-mail, or the news, or Facebook, or LinkedIn. Before you can say Jack Robinson, I have addressed all the items that seem more pressing at the time. The administrivia drains my creative juices like an arachnid sucking the liquid innards of its prey.

Here's the last example. Many big-time novelists like to work from early morning to mid-afternoon. At three or four o'clock, they go for a solitary walk to refresh, renew, and reflect. So for weeks, now, I've tried to follow a daily schedule built around this routine. But each day, when three o'clock rolls around, I surrender when confronted by a wind too blustery or a splatter of rain or a bowl of fresh popcorn.

Right now, for instance, it's 3:30 on a sunny, early spring afternoon. I have the beaches and woodland trails of Outer Cape Cod available outside my door. But a half hour ago—at three o'clock—I convinced myself that it's more important to write this blog post than to go rambling.

Whether it's sticking to a daily routine or a healthy diet or an exercise regimen, I have a hunch that I am not alone in my lack of self-discipline. Even Saint Paul admitted in his letter to the early church at Rome: "I do not do the good I want, but I do the evil I do not want."

# 90

## *How to Grow Your Brain*
## *Without Half-Trying*

Silence literally makes your brain bigger.

I just came across a 2013 study published in the journal *Brain Structure and Function*—about the effect silence had on the brains of mice. The scientists discovered that when the mice were exposed to two hours of silence per day they developed new cells in the hippocampus, a region of the brain associated with memory, emotion, and learning.

I served my writing apprenticeship in the city rooms of daily newspapers, so I'm no stranger to noise. I learned how to block out chatter, shouting, and random blasphemies while putting together a news story accurately and succinctly (well, at least succinctly). My ability to find a quiet place in my mind to write amid the cacophony proved contemporary French writer Charles de Leusse's thought that, "Noise hides the silence. It does not destroy the silence."

Here's what some other studies of silence show, as reported by science writer Rebecca Beris:

- Children who were exposed to noise developed a stress response that caused them to ignore the noise. These children, however, ignored not only harmful stimuli, but also stimuli they should be paying attention to—such as speech.
- If you live in a consistently noisy environment, you are likely to experience chronically elevated levels of stress hormones.
- Noise—even at levels that do not produce any hearing damage—causes stress and is harmful to humans.
- Two minutes of silence can prove to be more relaxing than listening to "relaxing" music.
- Noise harms performance at work and school, can decrease motivation and increase errors. The cognitive functions most strongly affected by noise are reading attention, memory, and problem solving.
- Children exposed to households or classrooms near airplane flight paths, railways or highways have lower reading scores and are slower in their development of cognitive and language skills.

I see silence as the default mode of existence. When God speaks, his language is silence. When he sculpts galaxies, sets planets spinning, blows up stars, or pokes a black hole into being, all is discharged in the utter silence of extraterrestrial space.

When it comes to inner space, however, the late Archbishop Fulton J. Sheen cut to the quick: "... noise is invoked to drown out the whisperings of conscience."

# 91

## *It's Not the Economy, Stupid*

Many years ago a little boy I was teaching was found hanged in his attic. They said it was an accident while playing. I've always wondered if maybe Marco, twelve years of age, had taken his own life.

I've thought of him often during the years, but never more than now, with the recent news that suicide among girls ten to fourteen years old has tripled.

The overall suicide rate rose by 24 percent from 1999 to 2014, and was particularly steep for women, according to a report by the National Center for Health Statistics.

What I find most dispiriting are the attempts of experts to explain what's behind the startling numbers. The experts are secularists seeking a secular answer to a transcendent matter.

Dr. Alex Crosby, for example, is with the Centers for Disease Control and Prevention. His studies of suicide go back to the 1920s and show that suicide is highest when the economy is weak. One of the highest rates in the country's modern history, he said, was in 1932, during the Great Depression.

Katherine Hempstead of the Robert Wood Johnson Foundation, in a PBS interview, agreed. But, she noted, suicide among young males is often impulsive—the result of a recent event, like a fight with a parent. She hinted that sometimes teens consider suicide cool.

Dr. Raj Raghunathan, at the University of Texas, says his research shows that supposedly successful people don't always make life choices that lead to happiness.

In an article in *The Guardian*, he said that after a reunion with his PhD classmates, he noticed that the more visible their achievements—work promotions, pay raises, fancy vacations, and big houses—the more unfulfilled and distracted they seemed overall.

Maybe we should look at some social trends of the past fifteen years or so—the period matching the increased rate of suicide by adolescent girls:

- Rap music and pornography that frame females as bitches, sluts, and whores
- Pressure on young girls to be thin, pretty, and sexually available— so boys will "like" them
- Widespread acceptance of casual sex with little mention of its emotional ramifications for girls

The results? Low self-esteem and self-hatred, because little girls can't live up to these expectations—magnified by bullying, which has careened out of control with the anonymity of online social media.

What else? States are hell-bent on adopting assisted-suicide legislation, and suicide is being suggested to adolescent girls in a way that had not been before.

We adults should be ashamed that we allow if not enable all this. Our mission is to give adolescents the moral, spiritual, and philosophical grounding for answers to the age-old questions of, "Who am I, Why am I here, Where am I going."

As one of my favorite poets, John Donne, wrote in *Meditation 17* way back in 1624:

*Any man's death diminishes me,*
*Because I am involved in mankind,*
*And therefore never send to know for whom the bell tolls;*
*It tolls for thee.*

When Bill Clinton ran for president in 1992, his manager hung a banner in the campaign war room: "It's the economy, stupid."

That thinking might get a fresh-faced politician elected. Economic or financial reversals might explain suicide by adults. But little girls do not kill themselves over the economy.

# 92

## It Must Be Spring

Those of us who live year-round here on Cape Cod don't pay much attention to spring, because we seldom actually see one. We maintain our winter rawness until at some point we start to sweat—and then we know it must be summer.

During April, for example, the average high was 52, the low 37. We had only twelve days recorded as "clear," and two of them had exceptionally high winds.

If it weren't for the arrival of the birds, which is now in full swing, we wouldn't know it's spring.

I like the poetry of Elizabeth Bishop, who wrote:

*All my life I have lived and behaved very much like a sandpiper, just running down the edges of different countries and continents, looking for something.*

Maybe this is why I feel an affinity for the birds of Cape Cod, and the way their birdsong occurs as if by magic when you least expect it.

The birds start their day before dawn—4 a. m. out here on the far-eastern boundary of eastern daylight saving time, where the native Wampanoag called themselves "children of the first light."

I don't know why the birds are so excited so early; all they have to look forward to is a breakfast of bugs. But after the quiet of winter here in Truro, fifty-plus miles out in the Atlantic Ocean, the birdsong of spring is very welcome.

During the cold months, just about the only birds we hear are crows. Their barking hardly qualifies as song, though. Cooing mourning doves also winter on Cape Cod, as do robins, but they are seldom seen and more seldom heard. Robins, in fact, have convinced most people that they are harbingers of spring.

Cape Cod is a flyway for more than 350 species of birds that trek between the Arctic and Antarctic. The Outer Cape—where my Truro home is—presents a geographic position (at midlatitudes and jutting into the Atlantic) that migrant birds find alluring. We also offer them an array of bird-welcoming habitats that make us a prime resting and feeding area. Lots of them remain for the entire summer: woodpeckers and whippoorwills, orioles and cardinals, bobwhites and finches.

Jo Knowles, author of *Jumping Off Swings*, takes a jaundiced view of all this:

> *I'm lying in my room listening to the birds outside. I used to think they sang because they were happy. But then I learned on a nature show they're really showing off. Trying to lure in some other bird so they can mate with it. Or let the other birds know not to get too close to their turf. I wish I never watched that show, because now all I think about is what those pretty sounds mean. And how they're not pretty at all.*

For my part, I don't care whether it's wooing or warring that the birds are up to. The chorus of their calls makes me happy. I join with "Lumberman's Poet" Douglas Malloch in proclaiming:

> *You have to believe in happiness, or happiness never comes. That's the reason a bird can sing. On his darkest day he believes in spring.*

Even after they leave in autumn, the echoes of their songs linger. Here's Thomas Bailey Aldrich in the nineteenth century:

> *What is more cheerful, now, in the fall of the year, than an open wood-fire? Do you hear those little chirps and twitters coming out of that piece of apple-wood? Those are the ghosts of the robins and bluebirds that sang upon the bough when it was in blossom last spring. . . . So I have singing birds all the year round.*

# 93

## *Children of the Dream*

I'll never forget the Memorial Day when my Uncle Paul smacked his little daughter across the face because she used a small American flag as a plaything.

It happened when my cousin and I were kids no more than seven or eight years old and the memory of World War II was still vivid for people like Uncle Paul, who himself had not served.

Back then, my family spent Memorial Day at the church cemetery, with the priest conducting a brief prayer service at the grave of each fallen soldier or sailor. There were so many. It took all day. And we kids, hot and thirsty under the sun, amused ourselves with made-up games—like playing with the little flags that were all around.

On this Memorial Day weekend, a time of holiday parades and picnics, I have to wonder if we still share the American Dream for which so many suffered and died.

We all are children of that dream, descendants of John Winthrop's vision of the Massachusetts Bay Colony as a place of limitless opportunity for material, social, and financial advancement.

Governor Winthrop's vision of his "City upon a Hill" was one in which individual ambition was to be tempered with charity and decency. It was to be a community whose citizens had the freedom to make the most of their lives by developing essential virtues—justice and mercy chief among them.

But this vision has degraded since he articulated it in 1630. The focus has shifted from community to self.

The American Dream we dream today is one of unquestioned access to unfettered personal freedoms. We won't have anybody tell us what we can or cannot do or think—unless we are already in agreement. We have ambition for and anticipation of self-satisfaction in every aspect of our public and private dealings and relationships.

And we won't have it any other way.

F. Scott Fitzgerald's 1925 novel, *The Great Gatsby*, has been called "the purest expression of America's promise of success." Even though the author was at the height of his fame, people hated the book and refused to buy it because it debunked the American Dream.

Fitzgerald's fame faded and he eventually sank into alcoholism and obscurity, with many of the 23,000 unread copies of *Gatsby* gathering dust in the publisher's warehouse.

In 1939, a year before Fitzgerald died, a movie was released that sentimentally but convincingly captured what America wanted to believe—despite the darkness of war that was descending on Europe. Its most memorable song, sung by a lost little girl:

*Somewhere over the rainbow*
*Skies are blue,*
*And the dreams that you dare to dream*
*Really do come true.*

In this new time of turmoil, perhaps we need to get back to our beginnings and remember that the American Dream is about more than ourselves alone. It's still a dream of ambition—but one tempered with charity and decency, justice, and mercy.

# 94

## *Something to Be Said*

There's something to be said about going it alone. With no one else partnering your life, you have both time without conversation and long spaces of silence. And in this dimension, you tend to notice things. For example, this week I posted on Facebook the following:

*I'm finding that living solo presents moments unnoticed when one's life is busily entwined with another's. This evening, the first time in perhaps a decade, I sat alone on my deck with wine and watched the sun sink into Cape Cod Bay. Scent of sea and aroma of sweet fern, fussing of birds nesting for the night, not a sound from so-troubled humankind. A door closes behind, a portal opens before.*

A few days later I posted a photo of my late wife's rosebush, which just burst into full bloom in this warm and dry Cape Cod June. Here's what I wrote:

*This rose bush was planted by Jo Anne's mother at their home in New Jersey, and Jo Anne grew up enjoying the flowers every June. When we built our Cape Cod house twenty years ago, Jo Anne planted a cutting below our bedroom window and the roses have bloomed beautifully ever since. I realized today that this is the first June she isn't here to welcome the new blossoms.*

As I said, in silence and solitude you tend to notice things.

Close to five hundred readers were engaged through these posts. Why did I receive such a sizable response?

I think that many of us are discovering a deep-seated craving for contemplation, which can be accomplished only in silence and solitude. Away from politicians' shouting and shrieking. Away from the havoc of exploding bombs that the media bring right into our homes. Away from iPhones, iTunes and I don't know what other ubiquitous and unrelenting sensory assaults.

And there are other, even more insidious invasions against our peace of mind. Thanks to Microsoft's recent purchase of LinkedIn, for instance, the Office software suite might have a new capability to unsolicitedly "suggest" an expert to connect with via LinkedIn to help with a task you're trying to complete.

Says Randall Stross, a professor of business at San Jose State University: "If I'm working in Word, I can't see why I'd welcome the intrusion of even a close friend, let alone a bot telling me about a stranger pulled from LinkedIn's database."

How's this for irony: Having started my day writing about our personal and societal need for tranquility, my next task is to finalize a scene in my novella, *Billy of the Tulips*, in which Billy and his father have a traumatic confrontation thick with shouting, cursing, and crying.

I need to finish the book before Microsoft starts intruding into my manuscript. So quiet, please—I'm writing.

# 95

## *A Bully and a Bigot*

Some years ago, a professor at Stanford University set up a mock prison on campus and recruited students to play roles as guards and prisoners. It was to be a two-week experiment, but within a few days the professor aborted the study because the student-guards turned vicious. To maintain power, they brutalized the student-prisoners whom they considered troublemakers. In like manner, some of the student-prisoners turned to collaboration with the student-guards in order to gain a scrap of control over their lives. The professor concluded that humans quickly learn to act according to their expectations of the roles they are given. This he called the Lucifer Effect.

I'm writing about this because after a week of nonstop news about the racial animosity gripping our society, I awoke at two this morning alarmed that the situation is unchanged—probably worsened—since I was a kid growing up in an industrial, blue-collar New Jersey city during the years that Puerto Ricans were first arriving in large numbers.

My father was a cop in that city. And a bully. I fictionalize him in a novel I'm completing:

> *Tony often came home at the end of his shift to describe his prowess at law enforcement. Like the dirty-talking woman he had to slam against a wall after he arrested her on a drunk and disorderly call. "She started swearing at me." he told Antoinette. "She had to learn ya' don't talk to a police officer that way." Or how he had kneed a young Puerto Rican in the groin hard enough to leave him doubled up on the floor of a holding cell.*
>
> *"Maybe he didn't know enough English to understand what you wanted," Antoinette said.*
>
> *"He was just making out that he didn't comprendo," Tony said. "I've seen him around. He's a wise-ass Spic. Always gives me this stare like he wants to knife me. That's how Spics are. They all carry knives. I opened the cell and gave him a little push from behind to get him to hop-to, and he turned around too fast, like he was gonna take a swing at me. So I shoved my knee up between his balls. He understood that pretty well."*

For my father, there seemed to be an endless supply of wise guys, drunks, and punks—both male and female—who didn't hop-to. He even made it a point to tell my mother and me how blacks have a particular stink about them when they perspire.

I didn't get it. I thought my Puerto Rican classmates in middle school were cool guys with whom I got along just fine. I was crazy for a dark-eyed Puerto Rican girl named Rita. And my best friend during those years was Lawrence Dalton—a Negro, as we called "them" back then.

If I indict my Dad for his wrongs, though, I also have to point an accusing finger at myself:

- When we were planning my wedding, my future in-laws refused to invite one of my friends because he was dating a Jamaican girl. Instead of insisting, I let it go.
- When I was a cub reporter earning a hundred dollars a week, I

drove a jalopy Cadillac. The police chief of one of the towns on my beat pulled up next to me at a gasoline station and called to me: "What are you doing in that nigger car?" Instead of writing a story about it, I let it go.

- When I was brand new at IBM in the late sixties and turning out the employee newspaper at one of their sites, the head of Personnel called me about doing a story on the fledgling diversity program there. He opened with: "We have to do something for the Boons." Instead of reporting him, I let it go.

Prejudice is a form of bullying. I realize today that my father succeeded in teaching me to be a racial bully—not in my overt actions, but by my cowardly silence, by my passive bigotry.

Maybe by getting out of bed in the middle of the night to write about it, I am finally standing up and trying in some small way to right what has been so terribly wrong for so terribly long.

# 96

## *Friends or Playmates?*

A perfect storm of three related coincidences this week has unnerved my until-now comfortable persona as a single, widowed man.

First was *The New York Times* story about Britain's growing awareness of loneliness as a serious public health issue. Researchers have found mounting evidence linking loneliness to physical illness and to functional and cognitive decline. Loneliness now eclipses obesity as a predictor of early death.

This is a situation of significance because roughly one in three people older than 65 lives alone. Fully half of Americans older than 85 live alone.

John T. Cacioppo, a professor at the University of Chicago who's been studying loneliness since the 1990s, compares loneliness to thirst, hunger or pain. "Denying you feel lonely makes no more sense than denying you feel hunger," he says.

The second coincidence was the publication of a new book titled *The Oxford Pictures*, demonstrating that loneliness is not the province of only the elderly.

Between 1968 and 1978, photographer Paddy Summerfield captured images of Oxford students in various states of isolation and uncertainty. What he sensed on the university campus was an atmosphere that mirrored how he, as a young man, felt about his own life when he took the photographs: "I was always outside everything. Often, I sensed a loneliness in the students I photographed. We were all lonely together."

The third component of my perfect storm was a conversation during which I suddenly realized that I have no friends to call on the spur of the moment and ask, "How about dinner tonight?" or "Feel like a movie?"

We're socialized at an early age about the critical importance of having friends. Consider this childhood ditty, of unknown origin:

*There are big ships,*
*There are small ships,*
*There are gold ships,*
*There are silver ships.*
*But there is no ship like friendship.*

Even before we've grown too big for the sandbox, we taste the devastation of being told by an irate playmate, "I'm not going to be your friend anymore!" We accept that "there is no happiness like that of being loved by your fellow creatures," as Charlotte Brontë wrote in Jane Eyre.

But it may take a lifetime of experience to differentiate a playmate from a friend.

I now feel in my bones, for example, my friendship with Vic. We were altar servers together in grade school, attended secondary school together, worked at *The New York Daily News* together, enjoyed simply driving around the New Jersey shore together on summer nights with hardly a word needed. He lives some 1,500 miles away these days, but all we have to do is pick up the phone and again be back together, with the summer breeze blowing into the open car windows and ruffling our hair.

I have been counseled that to elude loneliness at this point in my life I need to get involved in an activity or group where I can "make new friends" because almost all my familiars live far away—New York, Puerto Rico, California, Florida, Oregon.

So I'm exploring local church groups, library programs, the senior center, Hospice, The Manhood Project, Audubon, the Center for Coastal Studies.

But will doing this yield friends—or just playmates? Can I really expect to find at a senior center social a friendship like the deep, decades-long relationship I had with my wife? One that met Aristotle's definition of friendship as "a single soul dwelling in two bodies?"

She expressed our bond in the birthday card she gave me just weeks before she died:

*Dear Peter,*

*It's the best feeling knowing there's a strong, gentle hand that fits mine perfectly, and all I have to do is reach out and take it to feel safe, warm and loved.*

*All my love,*

*Me.*

Gaining future playmates for social company may be my "reward for finding one another out," as C. S. Lewis noted. But only in friendship do we possess "the instrument by which God reveals to each the beauties of all the others."

# 97

## *Remainders*

In the months since my wife's death, I've been slowly and meticulously disposing of her belongings, and shedding household items that accumulated during the decades we were together.

I'm learning that my living alone requires much less *stuff* than what was needed when we and our two daughters comprised a nuclear family of four.

There are three sets of dishes, for example. Three sets of dishes for two people—who aren't even kosher.

I followed my melancholy task of decluttering fifty years of marriage with a trip to Pittsburgh. My oldest grandson, Erik, received his doctorate in physical therapy from Duquesne University, and I wanted to be there to represent in a special way his late grandmother, who adored him.

The conjunction of these two antithetical events—the de-cluttering and the doctorate—hit me hard as I dropped my wife's beat-up old gardening Crocs into a trash bag: What is the true value of what remains after we leave our earthly life?

A *remainder* is defined as the part, number, or quantity that is left over.

In the publishing business, remainders are the books left unsold when demand has died.

When we depart, we leave behind not only personal possessions, but also unfinished work, unfulfilled ambitions, and unrealized dreams. The remainders of our lives.

But the word *remainder* has another meaning: a part that is still to come. The "remainder of the year" is an example.

This is the meaning that applies to the people on whom we've had special effect during our lives. It is here that what lingers of us applies in the most significant way.

Jo Anne's elegant clothes and jewelry, her collections of antique salt dishes, mid-century charm bracelets and Nancy Drew novels, her flower beds, and her precious koi—all are now trivial in light of her effect on the grandson who spent so many hours as a tyke in her care, who was so much the apple of her eye.

I'm proud of Erik's academic accomplishments. Even more, I'm gratified by what a sincere and caring young man he has become. And I am so aware of how much of Jo Anne remains in him.

# 98

## *The Worst Mistake*

Here's Andrew Solomon, writing in *The New Yorker* last year:

*The worst mistake anyone can make is to perceive anyone else as lesser. The deeper you look into other souls—and writing is primarily an exercise in doing just that—the clearer people's inherent dignity becomes.*

I disagree. I'd suggest that the worst mistake you can make is to perceive *yourself* as lesser.

Self-approval is a weighty opponent to one's psyche. Our society likes to slap labels on how we're perceived—especially negative ones. And we readily accept these labels. Especially the negative ones.

At this advanced stage of my life, however, I'm just now accepting the fact that I am a whole, a unity of many parts, a soul sustained by a loving God. And I'm learning to compartmentalize the competing components of my complex persona.

This means that when I sin, I am not evil. When I don't match up to expectations—my own or another's—I am not a loser. When I am betrayed, I am not a victim. As such, I am neither the lesser—nor the better—of anyone else. In fact, I am the only one, save my creator, who comprehends the wholeness of who I am.

I believe, therefore, that my role is not to judge, but to love. Starting with myself.

This isn't a new thought. Two thousand years ago, Saint Paul wrote to the Corinthians, "I do not even pass judgment on myself."

Truth be told, I have spent my life trying to please others in order to validate my anxious self. Among them:

- My father, who liked to remind me that I "couldn't fix a pimple on a mechanic's ass"
- My bosses at *The New York Daily News*, IBM, and Siemens, who seemed to breathe a different oxygen than I did
- My corporate clients, when I operated Executive Media, who sometimes saw me as waitstaff instead of business partner

Most significant and longest lasting was my wife, whose approval I sought in almost everything I did—personal or business.

In my unfamiliar role as widower, I'm finally recognizing that my wife is no longer here to approve or disapprove. I'm finally beginning to grasp the idea that only I, and my God, can validate the totality of who I am.

There is new freedom in this. Also the chance—and the challenge—to be truly my own.

# 99

## Julie's Story

*My younger daughter this week celebrated a birthday—her first since losing her mother to breast cancer. Julie wrote this brief remembrance in her honor. I was struck by the idea that, yes, each of us reaches a point in our lives when no one remains to remember the day we were born— what the weather was like, what time we arrived, what Mom was doing when the birth pangs began. So here is a chapter of Julie's life that she herself wrote. I offer her moving words so you can recall the story of your own children's birth and consider leaving them the gift of remembrance that my wife, Jo Anne, bequeathed to our daughter, Julie.*

A year ago, Mom called to wish me a Happy Birthday, as usual. And she started telling me the story of the day I was born: how she was at Woolworth's on a beautiful spring-like day (like today), buying buttons for a sweater she had just finished knitting, and felt a little something like she'd need to go to the hospital soon.

While she waited for Dad to come home from work, she made all the arrangements for someone to watch my sister, Wendy, while Dad took Mom to the hospital. And just a little while later, there I was.

When Mom called me a year ago, I started to tease her, telling the story along with her, because she'd told me the same story every year, on my birthday.

Then she told me why she kept telling the story: because when Grandpa had died (many years after Nana), she felt that no one in the world was left to remember the day she was born.

And she wanted me to remember "my story."

I felt about yay big for teasing her, because I finally understood why she told the story to me over and over and over.

Today I miss hearing my story one more time.

# 100

## A Letter to My Grandsons

*Another graduation season has come and gone and my three grandsons have taken another step ahead in their education: Erik with his spanking new doctorate in physical therapy from Duquesne. Connor with an undergraduate degree from Drexel prior to seeking a master's in psychotherapy, Andrew done with high school and headed for the University of Connecticut's pre-med program. They are embarking on life, while I am now old enough to be seriously thinking about my debarkation. What follows is my open letter to them.*

Good God Almighty, she was out of this world. The huge eyes, the sunshine smile, the little wiggle as she passed by in her trim red skirt.

Hold on, boys. I'm describing your grandmother! As I saw her on the day I met her.

My own grandfather fell for my grandmother because of a hat she wore to church one Sunday. In those days, the men sat on one side of the

Ukrainian church, the women on the other. Across the aisle from him, my grandmother stood out from the rest of the ladies. Just as your grandmother stood out at Fordham's School of Education, where the ratio of women to men was something like ten to one.

This was Romance.

Couples in the Romance stage move in together these days. Sort of a sociosexual test drive.

Then, living together or married, in a shorter time than you can imagine, Disillusionment comes.

Andy Warhol: "Romance is finding your fantasy in people who don't have it."

The painful thing is that, in your heart, you know Disillusionment is inevitable. There's nothing to be done about it. As Paul Murray writes in *The Mark and the Void:*

> *It's like when you find out your lover has been unfaithful: in one horrible instant everything she was to you, the whole beautiful enchantment, falls away, and you see her as she really is—mortal, machinating, tethered like everyone else to a little patch of space and time. And the worst of it is that you knew all along.*

But you can come to terms with the Disillusionment, compartmentalize the tedium, reach a comfortable stasis until, over the years, you finish each other's sentences. Even then you find that you can occasionally hurt each other in ways, small and large, that you never, ever dreamed you could.

I studied Latin under an old classics professor. When he emigrated from Europe, his PhD credentials were not recognized in this country, so he rolled up his sleeves and earned another from Columbia University. He was so smart that he wrote his doctoral dissertation entirely in Latin.

He used to give us a lot of grandfatherly advice to prepare us for life. My favorite: "Boys, when you meet a girl, don't look at her chest. Look at the back of her neck to see if it's clean."

I would tell you that in addition to the back of the neck of a potential life partner, look for shared spiritual beliefs, for these will nourish and sustain your dreams as a couple.

I know you guys are at a crossroads of belief. So many people you respect, including your teachers, scoff at faith. The media, the movies, your friends deride organized religion. It's no longer smart to have faith, much less be Catholic, thanks in large part to a clergy who betrayed us just as Judas did Jesus.

But can religion be one vast conspiracy that has successfully pressed on for thousands of years?

Literally hundreds of people were reported to have seen the resurrected Jesus. Did all of them lie?

Why did the original Apostles who ran for their very lives when Jesus was arrested return to fearless ministry—and all but one of them die for it?

Is every last one of the millions of miracles reported over the centuries a fraud?

In *Crux*, Dwight Longenecker recently wrote:

> *I come away with the opinion of Hamlet, that 'there are more things in heaven and earth than your philosophy has dreamt of.' There are enough inexplicable details, and enough unexplained coincidences, to make me conclude that behind and beneath the politics and power plays of this world there is another Player, another Plan and a greater Power.*

I cannot persuade you with my few words today, boys. And I can't put it in better words than Thomas Aquinas did seven hundred years ago: "To one who has faith, no explanation is necessary; to one without faith, no explanation is possible."

Here's something I think about often, and you guys should think about it, too: that basic religious and spiritual thought has remained essentially the same through the ages. But science is unrecognizable from what it was 3,500 years ago. Science changes and refutes itself daily. Science still hasn't decided if eggs are good for us or bad.

More significant than its vacillation about eggs, science to this day cannot understand how consciousness rises up from a lump of wet protein—our brain.

Writing in *The New York Times*, science writer George Johnson noted:

> *The human mind has plumbed the universe, concluding that it is precisely 13.8 billion years old. With particle accelerators like the Large Hadron Collider at CERN, scientists have discovered the vanishingly tiny particles, like the Higgs boson, that underpin reality. But there is no scientific explanation for consciousness—without which none of these discoveries could have been made.*

But you and I know why we have consciousness. We have a soul. We are creatures engineered for eternity.

Pigmented oils brushed onto canvas is what science sees. The Mona Lisa is what persons of soul see—the transcendent meaning of those pigments.

Empiricism stops short at the threshold of the transcendent, unequipped to enter.

But there's no reason why we humans cannot accept the transcendent, the sacred, and the consecrated. Because we are a soulful species unlike any other animal.

It's unfortunate that you are entering a world in which so much of the sacred has been desecrated.

Our society, for example, profanes the miracle of human life, mating without necessarily breeding. If a woman desires the life in her womb to blossom, she proudly calls it a baby, photographs its sonogram image, and gives it a name. If she chooses to believe otherwise, she dismisses the life within her as a tissue mass and flushes it away.

The consecrated state of life known as marriage is another example of something sacred that's been desecrated—relegated to "a piece of paper," demystified by pornography, profaned by the egocentrism of adultery.

My greatest consolation right now is that your grandmother left this life knowing that I loved her. On her deathbed she whispered to her daughters, "Daddy loves me."

Hearing those words makes me feel comforted that I have fulfilled in part the great commandment to "Love one another as I have loved you."

Jesuit priest Pierre Teilhard de Chardin—the French philosopher, paleontologist, and geologist who had a hand in the discovery of Peking Man—said that, "Joy is the infallible sign of the presence of God."

Now that your grandmother is gone, what I like to do these quiet mornings is sit silently by myself in church, where, I believe, God is present in a real way.

In doing this, I bridge the chasm between life and death, this world and the next, the physical and the metaphysical. While I am worshipping God in church, your departed grandmother, now beyond time and space, is also worshiping him. She and I are spiritually shoulder to shoulder before our God, she with him in the Paradise he promised, I before his same presence on the altar.

During these silent moments, I am as close to her as I can be.

And this is Joy.

# Sources and Notes

## Introduction

**xiii**

A discussion of thin places can be found on page TR10 of the New York edition of *The New York Times*, March 11, 2012, with the headline, "Where Heaven and Earth Come Closer."

For additional information about co-inherence see "The Concept of Co-inherence" in *The Writings of Charles Williams*.

Excerpts from *Courage to Pray* by Metropolitan Anthony Bloom. Copyright 1973 by Darton, Longman & Todd Ltd. Published by Vladimir's Seminary Press and Darton, Longman & Todd. Copyright 1984 by Vladimir's Seminary Press.

**xiv**

Dialog excerpt from "Our Town" in *Three Plays by Thornton Wilder* (New York: Bantam, 1972). Page 62. First presented in New York City at Henry Miller's Theatre, February 4, 1938.

**xv**

Excerpt from *The Twilight Zone* television series. (*Opening narration, Season 1*).

*Their Eyes Were Watching God* by Zora Neale Hurston. (J. B. Lippincott & Co., 1937).

## THE LADY OF THE DUNES

**6**

Lobur as quoted in "New Clues in Provincetown's Woman in the Dunes Case Point to Bulger Connection." Wickedlocal.com. (March 1, 2012).

## WTF!

**9**

*Bill Bernbach Said* by Bill Bernbach.

## STARSHIP COMMANDERS

**11**

Jim Lovell as told to the author.

## CORPORATE HARA-KIRI

**13**

*"Pepsi Launches First Global Campaign, 'Live For Now.'"* Press release by Pepsico, Purchase, NY (April 30, 2012).

## GODDESS OF THE HUNT

**19**

Nyad statistics from *The Scribner Encyclopedia of American Lives: Sports Figures* Vol.2, edited by Arnie Markoe. (New York, 2002).

**20**

Derivation of *nyad* from "The Ups and Downs of Living with a Con Artist." *Newsweek* 146.5 (August 1, 2005): 17.

## GATEWAYS

**21**

"Future Perfect" by Lia Purpura. Published in *The New Yorker*. (November 18, 2013).

For a discussion of string theory, see "A Universe Of 10 Dimensions" by Matt Williams, universetoday.com.

## LONELY, OR ALONE?

### 23

"Social Structural Factors to Perceptions of Relationship Quality and Loneliness: The Chicago Health, Aging, and Social Relations Study" by Louise C. Hawkley, Mary Elizabeth Hughes, Linda J. Waite, Christopher M. Masi. Ronald A. Thisted, John T. Cacioppo. *Journal of Gerontology.* (November 1, 2008).

### 24

Quotes cited in *Hopper's Places* by Gail Levin. Copyright 1985. Second edition, University of California Press.

Carter and Wolfe quotes from *God's Lonely Man.*

### 25

*The Eternal Now* by Paul Tillich. (Scribner, 1963).

## DARK

### 30

Serling excerpt from "Nothing in the Dark," *The Twilight Zone.* Closing narration. (Season 3, episode 16).

Van Gogh letter to his brother, Theo, 1888. Smithsonian.com.

Excerpt from *The Hobbit: The Desolation of Smaug.*

*The Little Flowers of St. Francis of Assisi.*

## LIGHT

### 31

Thurber excerpt from "Where Heaven and Earth Come Closer." *The New York Times*, New York edition. Page TR10. (March 11, 2012).

**32**

Hoffmann as quoted in *Readings in American art, 1900-1975* by Barbara Rose. (Praeger, 1975). Page 117.

Fiore excerpt from *Artists* magazine, 2008.

## THE ECOLOGY OF SELF

**34**

"Egalitarianism, Housework and Sexual Frequency in Marriage." *The American Sociological Review.* (February 2013).

## LIGHTING THE MATCH

**36**

Excerpts from *Muhammad Ali* by Felix Dennis. (Miramax Books, 2003). Page 100.

*Within a Budding Grove, Madame Swann at Home.* ljhammond.com/proust.

**37**

1980 USA Olympic hockey team coach as quoted in *Sports Illustrated* online site.

## THE SLOWNESS OF TIME

**42**

"European grandparents' solicitude: Why older men can be relatively good grandfathers." By K. Knudsen. (*Acta Sociologica*, 2012).

John Clarke writes from his family's Kentucky farm.

## THE SOUNDS OF SILENCE

**44**

*Paul Simon: A Life* by Marc Eliot. (John Wiley and Sons, 2010).

## Born into Eternity

**47**
*Seduction of the Minotaur* by Anais Nin, 1961.

## Star Stuff

**49**
*Contact* by Carl Sagan. (Simon and Schuster, 1985).
*Cosmos, 5 min 15 sec.*

## Privacy, Pornography, Paradox

**54**
Pitt's speech against the Cider Bill of 1763.
**55**
2017 Facebook statistics from statista.com.
Intimate content statistics from marketwatch.com.
Statistics from facebook.com and a link to Damon Brown's blog.
**56**
*Evangelii Gaudium* by Pope Francis. (Libreria Editrice Vaticana, 2013).

## Fashionable or Foolish?

**58**
"Best & Worst Dressed at the 2014 Teen Choice Awards." (Eonline. com).
"Church Ladies and Hats a Thing of the Past." *Washington Post.* (April 7, 2012).

## Adam's Curse

**60**
*Consciousness: Confessions of a Romantic Reductionist* by Christof Koch. The MIT Press; 1st edition. (March 9, 2012).

**62**

Excerpt from *National Geographic*. (September 9, 2014).

Duell referenced in "About those 2012 Predictions" by Peggy Noonan. *The Wall Street Journal*. (December 28, 2012).

## Once Upon a Time

**66**

*Obama Power* by Jeffrey C. Alexander and Bernadette N. Jaworsky. (Polity, April 2014).

**67**

"Storytelling That Moves People." *Harvard Business Review*. (June 2003). *Rhetoric* by Aristotle.

## Cookie-Cutter People

**72**

*Coco Chanel: Her Life, Her Secrets* by Marcel Haedrich. (Little, Brown, 1971).

**73**

Excerpt from "How Not to Turn Away the Next Steve Jobs." Cal Entertainment. (April 2013).

## A Life in Black and White

**77**

Excerpt from *The Second Sex* by Simone de Beauvoir. *On ne naît pas femme: on le devient* translated and edited by H. M. Parshley. (New York: Knopf, 1954).

## Family Candy

**81**

Lewis Black video clip at: https://www.youtube.com/watch?v=VU6S3-cXtKs.

**82**

Excerpt from "A Cultural History of Candy." *Smithsonian.* (October 29, 2010).

## Psychogeography

**85**

Vladimir Strelnitski, director of the Maria Mitchell observatory, calculated on New Year's Day 2000 that Nantucket—an island—saw first light at least one minute earlier than Maine. National Public Radio "Morning Edition." (December 31, 2010).

Joseph Addison: *Spectator.* (No. 387).

## Bic Generation

**91**

"Divorce Is Actually on the Rise and It's the Baby Boomers' Fault." *Washington Post.* (March 27, 2014).

Report at www.samhsa.gov/homelessness-programs-resources/hpr-resources/child-homelessness-growing-crisis

## All Talk

**94**

"Unfolding Language, Unfolding Life" Interview by Krista Tippett. (*On Being* podcast, 2016).

*Recent Experiments in Psychology* by Leland Whitney Crafts, Théodore Christian Schneirla, and Elsa Elizabeth Robinson. (1950).

**95**

www.poemhunter.com attributes the quote to Montessori in *The Absorbent Mind.* (1949). Chapter 1.

## Nothing On

**97**

*This Book is Not FOR SALE* by Jarod Kintz.

The *Dyer's Hand* and *Other Essays*, in "The Poet and the City," (New York: Random House, 1962).

## Voluntary Madness

**101**

*Nihil aliud esse ebrietatem quam voluntariam insaniam* from *Epistulae Morales ad Lucilium,* Letter LXXXIII: On Drunkenness, line 18.

**103**

Nietzsche quote from goodreads.com.

## Victoria's Sleazy Secret

**105**

"Victoria's Secret will not make mastectomy bras." CBS News. (May 21, 2013, 6:02 PM).

## Operator, I've Been Disconnected

**108**

"An Ideal Childhood: Strangers in a Strange Land." *Tesla: Inventor of the Electrical Age* by W. Bernard Carlson (Princeton University Press, 2013). Page 13.

## Saints and Poets, Maybe

**110**

*Transparency* by Ken Sanes. (www.transparencynow.com).

## Simon Says

**113**

For a comprehensive description of the game: www.wikipedia.org/wiki/Simon_Says.

Excerpt from www.instyle.com/news/rachel-roy-advises-against-hand-hips-pose.

## They Take So Much with Them

**115**

Excerpt from *Here and Now* by Henri Nouwen.

## The Hunt for Happiness

**120**

Genesis 3:4-5 (NAB).

Matthew 11:29 (NAB).

"Stoicism." *The New Yorker.* (February 2, 2015).

**121**

*Epistulae Morales ad Lucilium, Letter XLVIII.*

## Robots 1, Humans 0

**128**

Martin Heidegger, "The Question Concerning Technology," *Basic Writings.* Ed. David Farrell Krell (Harper & Row, 1977). Page 287.

"Anti-Internet Movement Is Needed Says Expert." Gelernter interview with *Deutsche Welle.* (January 7, 2010).

## All It Takes

**129**

Leviticus 19:2 (NAB).

Babylonian Talmud, tractate. Shabbat 31a.

Description of Hall of Maat from Ancient Egypt Online.

**130**

Man under judgment as quoted by Simone Weil in *Awaiting God*, Fresh Wind Press; First Edition–New Translation edition, December 11, 2012.

Matthew 22: 37-40 (NAB).

Weil, *Awaiting God*.

## NUMBER ONE AND NUMBER TWO

**132**

The 2011 study for *Advertising Age* can be found at adage.com.

"How I Did It: Aflac's CEO Explains How He Fell for the Duck" by Daniel P. Amos. *Harvard Business Review*. (January 2010).

"How the Insurance Industry Got Into a \$4 Billion Ad Brawl" by E. J. Schultz. *Advertising Age*. (February 21, 2011).

"Flo's Progressive Evolution: 100th Ad Starring the Insurance Girl Launched This Week" by Ashley Rodriguez. *Advertising Age*. (November 12, 2014).

## UNIFORMS ARE SUPPOSED TO BE UNIFORM

**135**

Sue Wicks quote from brainyquote.com

**136**

Ryne Sandberg fielding statistic from chicago.cubs.mlb.com.

"Baseball Hall of Fame Induction Speech" by Ryne Sandberg. Cooperstown, NY. (July 31, 2005).

Joe Torre quote from time.com.

Tommy Lasorda excerpt from Baseball Almanac.

*This Book Is Not FOR SALE* by Jarod Kintz. (2011).

## COOKING FOR ONE

**138**

"Buddhist mindful eating practices enter the mainstream" by Sachi Fujimori, *The* (Bergen County, NJ) *Record*. (May 28, 2012).

## Why, Women?

**141**

Lewis website: http://womenshistory.about.com/od/mythsofwomenshistory/a/bra_burning.htm

Excerpt from "#NotGuilty: A letter to my assaulter" at cherwell.org.

**142**

"Helen Hunt Says Women In Hollywood Are 'F*cked'." huffingtonpost.com. (May 1, 2015).

"Where I Lived, and What I Lived For," *Walden*, Ch. 2, by Henry David Thoreau. (New York: Penguin Classics, 1986). Page 134.

## The Next-Larger Context

**145**

Biondi speech before ROLM Corporation recognition event, 1991.

"*AD* Remembers the Extraordinary Work of Eliel and Eero Saarinen." *Architectural Digest*. (July 31, 2014).

## The Coywolves of Cape Cod

**146**

Coywolf information from *The* (Westchester County, NY) *Journal News*, Massachusetts SPCA, *Toronto Star* (August 15, 2009), "Good Morning Gloucester" blog (3/26//2013), and *Discovery News* (2009).

## A Father's Day Gift to Women

**150**

Mollie Marti, J. D., Ph. D., quote from *Walking with Justice*. (Greenleaf Book Group Press, 2012).

## To Correct the Past

**152**

"Growing Pains at UC." *San Francisco Chronicle*. (November 15, 1964).

"How Old Are Silicon Valley's Top Founders? Here's the Data" by Walter Frick. *Harvard Business Review*. (April 3, 2014).

**153**

"Achievements by the very young: Part Three" from *What the Dog Saw* by Malcolm Gladwell. (Little, Brown, 2009).

**154**

*And Madly Teach: A Layman Looks at Public School Education* by Mortimer Brewster Smith. (1949). Page 27.


## For Better, for Worse

**155**

Rachael Hills interview in *The Guardian*: "The Sex Myth: Why we're not talking about not getting laid," August 4, 2015.


## A Millennial Pop Quiz

**158**

*Lectures in America* published January 1, 1985, by Beacon Press (MA). First published 1935.

*Investor's Business Daily*. (October 17, 2000).


## The Assault on Architecture

**162**

*The Hunchback of Notre-Dame*, Book III, 1. Notre Dame. (New York: Signet Classic, 1965) translated by Walter J. Cobb.


## Yada Yada Yada

**164**

"Professor uses 'Seinfeld' characters to teach Rutgers medical students about psychiatry." nj.com. (January 2, 2015).

## Gaudeamus, Igitur?

**167**

"What Is the Point of College?" *The New York Times Magazine.* (September 13, 2015).

"How to Live Wisely." *The New York Times.* (July 31, 2015).

## Three Women

**169**

Tagore quote cited by BrainyQuote.com, Xplore Inc, 2016.

## We Are Song

**170**

See the Department of Education website for full information about the Act: http://www2.ed.gov/policy/elsec/leg/esea02/index.html.

**171**

NAMM Foundation-funded (National Association of Music Merchants), nationwide study of 1,000 teachers and 800 parents.

Kreeft's talk on "Happiness" given in various places at various times. Transcript at Catholic Education Resource Center.

## The Zombie Muffin of Provincetown

**173**

Executive Summary in the 1999 report of the World Health Organization: "On the basis that azodicarbonamide is a human asthmagen and that the concentrations required to induce asthma in a non-sensitive individual or to provoke a response in a sensitive individual are unknown, it is concluded that there is a risk to human health under present occupational exposure conditions. The level of risk is uncertain; hence, exposure levels should be reduced as much as possible."

*In Defense of Food: An Eater's Manifesto* by Michael Pollan, Penguin Books; 1 edition (April 28, 2009).

Jud to Louis: "Maybe I did it because kids need to know that sometimes dead is better." *Pet Sematary* by Stephen King, Doubleday & Co.; 1st edition (1983).

## COAT OF MANY COLORS

**174**
Genesis 37:3 (NAB).

**175**
Andrew Lloyd Webber's Really Useful Group posted on June 29, 2007: "*Joseph and the Amazing Technicolor Dreamcoat* was first performed at Colet Court in South West London nearly 30 years ago. Since then the musical's popularity has grown due to the countless school productions which have been staged. It is estimated that the show has been performed in nearly 20,000 schools and local theatres, involving 700,000 performers of all ages, and with an audience in excess of nine million. Today there are nearly 500 school and amateur productions each year in the UK."

Address by Vice President Hubert H. Humphrey, Commencement Exercises, Fordham University, New York, NY, June 9, 1965.

## WHY SO LONELY?

**177**
SingularityHUB.com: Cisco predicts "a 25% annualized decrease in price to connect between 2012 and 2020 and a matching 25% annualized increase in connectivity. That means we can expect 50 billion connected things by 2020, with 50% of those connections happening in the final three years of the decade."

The NSF report is summarized in "The Loneliness of American Society" by Janice Crouse Shaw, *American Spectator*. (May 18, 2014).

**178**
*Laudato Si*: IV. Decline in the quality of human life and the breakdown of society.

"How technology is changing our likes and loves" by Kate Bussmann, *The Telegraph*. (December 30, 2013).

"The Effect Of Technology On Relationships" by Alex Lickerman, M. D., *Psychology Today*. (June 8, 2010).

"The Loneliness of American Society" by Janice Crouse Shaw, *American Spectator*. (May 18, 2014.)

## GREAT EXPECTATIONS

### 183

Philippians 4:11 (NAB).

## LETTER FROM THE DESERT

### 190

Mark 1:35 (NAB)

William of Saint-Thierry (c.1085–1148), monk, *Meditations IV, 10-11* (trans. ©Cistercian Publications, Inc. 1970).

### 191

*Cithara* magazine's twentieth-anniversary issue devoted to Merton. (May 1981).

"The Art of Fiction No. 69." Gabriel García Márquez interviewed by Peter H. Stone. *Paris Review*. (Winter 1981).

*A Defense of Poetry*, Paragraph 12, Percy Bysshe Shelley. (1821).

## THE SINISTER SIDE OF CHRISTMAS

### 193

"Spectral pleasures" by Michel Faber, *The Guardian*. (December 23, 2005).

Matthew 2:18 (NAB).

## Exits and Entrances

**196**

*Livius, Articles on Ancient History.*

**197**

*Uncoupling: Turning Points in Intimate Relationships* by Diane Vaughan. (Published September 5, 1990, by Vintage). First published 1986.

*Broken Open: How Difficult Times Can Help Us Grow* by Elizabeth Lesser. (Published June 14, 2005, by Villard). First published May 4th 2004.

## Slack Tide

**199**

"Vassa," *Encyclopaedia Britannica*

*Retreat Finder* online directory lists 2,569 retreats.

## What We Learn from Turtles

**200**

Cape Cod geographic profile from *Visit New England* online site.

**201**

*Their Eyes Were Watching God* by Zora Neale Hurston. (J. B. Lippincott & Co., 1937).

## Fear Is a Color

**204**

*Fighting the Good Fight* by George W. Rutler. (Sunlit Uplands, 2016). Luke 3:16 NAB).

Saint Bernard's *Sermon 82 in Cantica* quoted in *The Silent Life* by Thomas Merton. (Farrar, Straus and Giroux).

## The Hardest Love

**207**

Derrida's actual quote: " . . . forgiveness forgives only the unforgiveable." *On Cosmopolitanism and Forgiveness*. (London: Routledge, 2001).

Lucy Allais in "On Forgiveness" podcast by *Philosophy Bites*. (January 4, 2015).

**208**

*Sweet Wind, Wild Wind* by Elizabeth Lowell. Copyright 1987. (Silhouette Paperback).

*Prayer: Seeking the Heart of God* by Blessed Teresa of Calcutta with Bro. Roger.

Pope Francis impromptu press conference as quoted in *The New York Times*. (July 29, 2013).

*The Irony of American History* by Reinhold Niebuhr. Copyright 1984, (Scribner Book Company. Originally published in 1952).

## Going It Alone

**209**

*Pensées*, 9. *Diversions*. (Published 1662).

**210**

*The Power of Myth*. (Anchor, May 18, 2011).

*Conversation and Self-Sufficiency in Plato* by A. G. Long. (Oxford University Press, 2013).

"I never found the companion that was so companionable as solitude." *Walden*, or, *Life in the Woods* by Henry David Thoreau. (Published 1854).

*On Solitude* by Michel de Montaigne.

**211**

Matthew 6:6 (NAB).

## SUCCUBUS ON MY CHEST

### 212

Dialogue excerpt from *45 Years*. (Released December 2015)

### 213

"Why You Blame Yourself for Bad Relationships—and How to Stop" by Dr. Craig Malkin. *Psychology Today*. (May 11, 2012).

"Letting Go of Blame" by Mike Robbins. *Huffington Post*. (April 18, 2011).

Eleanor Roosevelt as quoted in *Reader's Digest*. (September 1940).

Bryant McGill quote from his website.

Debasish Mridha as quoted by Goodreads.

### 214

Luke 4:23 (NAB).

## BEST FRIENDS

### 215

Simone de Beauvoir excerpt from *Les Belles Images* by Simone de Beauvoir. Copyright 1986 by Gallimard, originally published in 1966.

### 216

"Be Mine? Why It's Smart to Court Your Friends" by Ann Friedman. *New York Magazine*. (October 24, 2013).

"How Are Men's Friendships Different from Women's?" by Ronald E. Riggio, Ph.D. (*Psychology Today*, October 9, 2014). Dr Riggio references "Asymmetries in the friendship preferences and social styles of men and women" by Jacob M. Vigil, 2007.

## FROM DARKNESS, LIGHT

### 218

"Over the Rainbow" music by Harold Arlen and lyrics by Yip Harburg. Written for the movie *The Wizard of Oz* (1939) and sung by Judy Garland.

Genesis 1:3 (NAB).

*A Grief Observed* by N.W. Clerk (pseudonym for C.S. Lewis). Copyright 1961 by Faber and Faber.

**219**

A saying variously attributed to Native Americans, Cherokee Nation, Tibetan Buddhism, or Ralph Waldo Emerson.

## "I Wish to Die for that Man"

**221**

Kolbe's story as told by Louis Bulow at fatherkolbe.com.

Aristotle as quoted by Diogenes Laërtius in *The Lives and Opinions of Eminent Philosophers* translated by C. D. Yonge; Henry G. Bohn, 1853, bi. V, sec. 18, p. 187, as reported in Bartlett's, page 77.

Aquinas's discussion of faith can be found in his *Summa Theologiae*.

Marcel quote cited in *Stanford Encyclopedia of Philosophy*, revised March 2016.

## Dueling with Ghosts

**222**

*The Haunting of Hill House* by Shirley Jackson. (Viking Press 1959).

**223**

Lao Tzu from The Quotepedia.

*The Blue Castle*, by L.M. Montgomery, Chap 19.

## Soufflé, Testosterone, and I

**225**

Facebook post by the James Beard Foundation.

**226**

Child quoted in *The* [San Jose] *Mercury News*, August 6, 2012.

*Home Cooking: A Writer in the Kitchen* by Laurie Colwin. (Vantage Books, 2010).

## THE GOOD THAT I WOULD

**228**
Romans 7:19 (NAB).

## HOW TO GROW YOUR BRAIN WITHOUT HALF-TRYING

**229**
De Leusse's thought in the original: *Le bruit cache le silence. Il ne détruit le silence.*

**230**
"Science Says Silence Much More Important To Our Brains Than Thought" by Rebecca Beris. lifehack.org.

Sheen's full thought from *The Angel's Blackboard/Words of Grace*: "Our world is one of speed in which intensity of movement is a substitute for lack of purpose; where noise is invoked to drown out the whisperings of conscience; where talk, talk, talk gives the impression that we are doing something when really we are not; where activity kills the self-knowledge won by contemplation."

## IT'S NOT THE ECONOMY, STUPID

**231**
Crosby's research cited in "Suicides in the U.S. Climb After Years of Declines." *The Wall Street Journal.* (April 22, 2016).

**232**
"How To Be Happy: Follow These Five Easy Steps" by Raj Raghunathan. *The Guardian.* (April 23, 2016).

## IT MUST BE SPRING

**234**
*Words in Air–The Complete Correspondence between Robert Lowell and Elizabeth Bishop,* edited by Thomas Travisand with Saskia Hamilton (2008).

**235**

*Jumping Off Swings* by Jo Knowles. (Candlewick, 2009). Page 180.

**236**

*Miss Mehetabel's Son* by Thomas Bailey Aldrich. (Fili-Quarian Classics, July 12, 2010).

## Something to Be Said

**240**

"Why LinkedIn Will Make You Hate Microsoft Word" by Randall Stross. *The New York Times*. (June 17, 2016).

## Friends or Playmates?

**244**

"Researchers Confront an Epidemic of Loneliness" by Katie Hafner. *The New York Times*. (September 5, 2016).

**245**

*The Oxford Pictures* by Paddy Summerfield, (Dewi Lewis Publishing, 2016). Quote from his website.

*Jane Eyre* by Charlotte Bronte, Chapter 22.

**246**

Aristotle quote from *Lives and Opinions of Eminent Philosophers* by Diogenes Laertius.

*The Four Loves* by C.S. Lewis. (HarperCollins Publishers Ltd, 2002). First published in 1960.

## The Worst Mistake

**249**

"Advice for Young Writers" by Andrew Solomon. *The New Yorker*. (March 11, 2015).

**250**

1 Corinthians 4:3 (NAB).

## A Letter to My Grandsons

**254**

*The Philosophy of Andy Warhol (From A to B and Back Again)* by Andy Warhol. (Harvest, April 6, 1977).

**255**

"Fatima proves that beyond politics and power, there's another Player" by Fr. Dwight Longenecker. *CRUX, an independent Catholic news site.* (May 13, 2016).

**256**

"Science of Consciousness Conference Is Carnival of the Mind" by George Johnson. *The New York Times.* (May 17, 2016).

**257**

"The Most Infallible Sign" by James Martin, S. J. *America, The Jesuit Review.* (April 02, 2007).

# *Photo Credits*

# About the Author

**PETER W. YAREMKO** has written for corporations throughout North and South America, Europe and Asia/Pacific. With a New York City journalism background, he headed communications for IBM and Siemens businesses, and founded a corporate communication practice now in its third decade of operation. The range of his writing includes speeches for CEOs and board chairs, film and video scripts, business theater continuity, advertising and sales promotion copy, and magazine writing and editing. He has taught college and corporate writing classes, and is author of four non-fiction books, a novella, and a novel in development. At various stages in his life, Mr. Yaremko also has played roles as a puppet, a pauper, a pirate, a poet, a pawn and a king. His blog: www.peterwyaremko.com.

Made in United States
Orlando, FL
05 December 2021

11161360R20165